THE COLLAPSE OF ZIMBABWE IN THE WAKE OF THE 2000-2003 LAND REFORMS

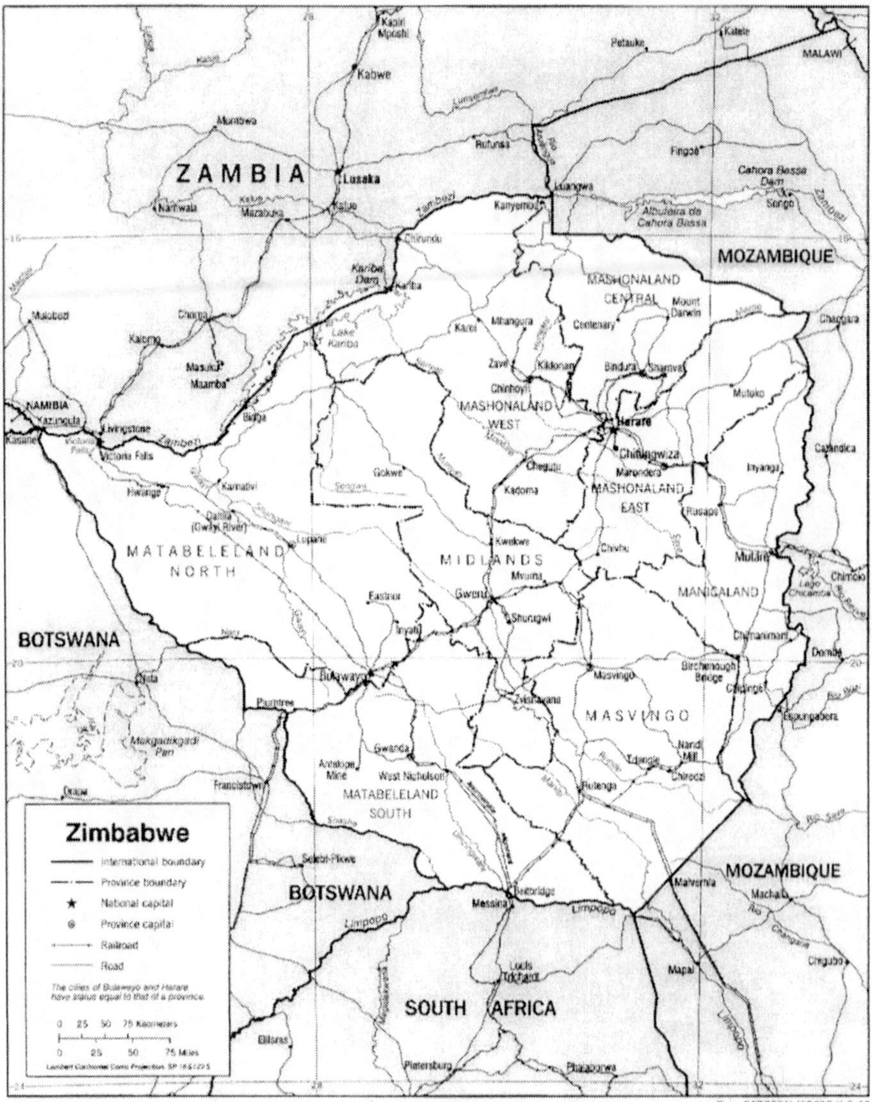

Base 802836AI (C00254) 3-02

Source: Central Intelligence Agency, U.S.A.

THE COLLAPSE OF ZIMBABWE IN THE WAKE OF THE 2000-2003 LAND REFORMS

Craig Richardson

Studies in African Economic and Social Development
Volume 24

The Edwin Mellen Press
Lewiston•Queenston•Lampeter

Library of Congress Cataloging-in-Publication Data

Richardson, Craig, 1962-
The collapse of Zimbabwe in the wake of the 2000-2003 land reforms / Craig Richardson.
p. cm. -- (Studies in African economic and social development ; v. 24)
Includes bibliographical references and indexes.
ISBN 0-7734-6366-6 (hd.)
1. Zimbabwe--Economic conditions--1980- 2. Right of property--Zimbabwe. 3. Zimbabwe Farmers Union. I. Title. II. Series.

HC910.R523 2004
330.096891'051--dc22

2004040266

This is volume 24 in the continuing series
Studies in African Economic and Social Development
Volume 24 ISBN 0-7734-6366-6
SAESD Series ISBN 0-88946-514-2

A CIP catalog record for this book is available from the British Library

Front cover: The Great Ruins of Zimbabwe
Courtesy of Serena Bowles

The Edwin Mellen Press
Box 450
Lewiston, New York
USA 14092-0450

The Edwin Mellen Press
Box 67
Queenston, Ontario
CANADA L0S 1L0

The Edwin Mellen Press, Ltd.
Lampeter, Ceredigion, Wales
UNITED KINGDOM SA48 8LT

Printed in the United States of America

Dedicated to my parents,

Lucy Richardson and Barrie Richardson

Contents:

List of Tables vi
List of Figures and Photographs vii
Acknowledgements ix

Preface by Hernando de Soto xiii

Introduction 1

Chapter 1.
The Critical Importance of Property Rights

A Short History 11
Literature Review on Property Rights and Economic Growth 14
The Link Between Property Rights and Growth 15
How Modulating Property Rights Affects the Value of Land 20

Chapter 2.
Zimbabwe's History and Government Protection of Property Rights

History of Property Rights in Zimbabwe 27
The Path of the New Mugabe Government 33
A Focus on Land Reform 35
Intimidation of the Media and Increasing Isolation 43
The Structure of the Government 44

Chapter 3.
Conflicts Over Land: The History and Structure of the Agricultural Sector

Overview 47
A Brief History Since 1965 48
Differences in Land Ownership Prior To
Land Seizures of 2000-2003 50
Other Complexities in Communal Property Right Laws. 54
Limits on Property Rights, and Enforcement 56
The Importance of Water 60

Chapter 4.
Government Agricultural Policies: What Happened?

Overview 63
The Role of Government Pricing Policy 63
Evaluating the Outcomes of Economic Reforms 67
Was the Drought to Blame? 70
Sharp Changes in Agricultural Production 75

Chapter 5.
The Foreign Exchange and Monetary Crises

Where Did the Hard Currency Go? 85
Wealth in Mining Operations 92
Driving Forces Behind the Rising Deficits 98
Tempting Target: The Reserve Bank of Zimbabwe 102

Chapter 6.
Education, Population and Health Care: From Highs to Lows

History of Education 107
Population Trends 113
Health Infrastructure, and AIDS 115

Chapter 7.
The Labor Market and Women's Role in it

The Structure of the Labor Force 125
The Predicament of Women in Zimbabwe 130

Chapter 8.
Lessons Learned From Nicaragua, Consequences, and Conclusions

Some Intriguing Parallels with Nicaragua 135
The Consequences of Insecure Property Rights 142
Room for Optimism: A Roadmap for the Future 143

Chapter Notes 149
Bibliography 159
Name Index 167
Subject Index 169

List of Tables

		Page
Table 2.1.	Key Legislative Acts and Events Affecting Land and Property Rights in Zimbabwe.	42
Table 3.1.	Differences in Farming Area by Type of Farmer, Prior to 2000	59
Table 3.2.	Commercial and Communal Agricultural Production	60
Table 4.1.	Evolution of Zimbabwean Policies, Fiscal Years 1990-1995	69
Table 4.2.	Comparing Droughts in Zimbabwe	74
Table 4.3.	Differences in Yields and Production Between Communal and Commercial Farms	76
Table 4.4	Estimated Total Production, Large Scale Commercial Sector	82
Table 4.5.	The Loss in Agricultural Revenue, and Wealth From Commercial Farmland 1997-2003	83
Table 5.1	Zimbabwe Mineral Production, Prices and Total Revenue	96
Table 6.1.	A Comparison of Males vs. Females in Zimbabwe's Tertiary Educational Institutions, 2000	111
Table 6.2.	Population Size By Ethnic Group, 1901 to 1982	114
Table 6.3.	Health Expenditures as a Percentage of GDP, 1960 vs. 1986	118
Table 7.1.	Labor Market Classifications, By Sex	129
Table 8.1.	Nicaragua: Inflation and GDP Growth, 1984-2000	137

List of Figures

	Page
Figure A. Zimbabwe: Changes in GDP Growth, from 1981-2003	3
Figure B. Zimbabwe: Anatomy of a Collapse	10
Figure 1.1. The Relationship Between Property Rights and Growth	25
Figure 4.1. Rainfall vs. GDP for Zimbabwe: 1981-2003	72
Figure 4.2. Changes in Areas Planted For Maize, Commercial Farms	77
Figure 4.3. Percent Changes in Commercial Farming Production: 2000-2003	80
Figure 4.4. Value of Commercial Agricultural Production, in millions of dollars	84
Figure 4.5. Total Imputed Wealth of Commercial Farmland, 1997-2003.	84
Figure 5.1. Official and Parallel Exchange Rates	87
Figure 5.2. Zimbabwe's Plunging Current Account	89
Figure 5.3. Total Gross Reserves Held By Zimbabwe Government	93
Figure 5.4. Declining Reserves of Gold	95
Figure 5.5. Government Spending Outpaces Tax Revenue	99
Figure 5.6. Ever-growing National Debt	100
Figure 5.7. Sources of Income to the Zimbabwean Government	101
Figure 5.8. Consumer Price Inflation 1998-2003	105
Figure 5.9. Money Supply Growth 1997-2002	105
Figure 6.1. Plunging Life Expectancy	118
Figure 6.2. HIV Seroprevalence for Zimbabwean Pregnant Women 1990-97	120
Figure 6.3. Knowledge of Ways to Prevent AIDS, 1998	123
Figure 8.1. Nicaragua: GDP Growth Rates 1984-2000	140

List of Photographs (center of book)

Photo 1. Satellite photo of Africa, highlighting Zimbabwe
Photo 2. Satellite photo of Zimbabwe, with administrative boundaries
Photo 3. Satellite photo of Zimbabwe; a closer look at the land degradation differences by type of farming methods

Acknowledgements

This book has represented an intriguing intellectual journey for me. Without a number of people there to influence, guide and challenge me, it would not have happened. For all of them and any others I have not named, I am extremely grateful. Susan Cochrane, at the Population and Human Resources Division of the World Bank, is responsible for the genesis of this book. While working at the Bank in 1990, Dr. Cochrane assigned me the task of writing a comprehensive background paper on Zimbabwe, and in doing so, subsequently ignited my interest in this fascinating country. Her warm and supportive feedback stayed with me, and was one of the reasons why I used that paper as a launch pad for writing this book nearly thirteen years later.

Neil Wright, the chief economist for Zimbabwe's Commercial Farmers' Union, was extremely generous with his time, sending me long and detailed comments on my earlier drafts, as well as providing me with primary agricultural economic data. This data was crucial in making a number of key points in the book. Gerry Patterson, President of the Commercial Farmers' Union, also helped me understand the key aspects of land titling and equity markets. Heartnear Dumbu, of the Department of Meteorology in the government of Zimbabwe, sent me hard-to-find rainfall data in an extremely timely fashion. Hernando de Soto, of the Institute for Liberty and Democracy in Peru deserves my special thanks for writing *Mystery of Capital*, which helped me focus on property rights as a key linchpin for free markets. I greatly thank him for his interest in this project. In addition, Milton Friedman's interest in my work was flattering, to say the least; his writings, both in style and in substance, have always served as great inspiration to me. I truly appreciate the time he spent reading a section of this book, and his positive feedback.

Art Goldsmith, of Washington and Lee University, invited me to present my findings to his economics class, and I greatly benefited from the interaction of him and his students. Shyama Wickramaaratchi, a student at Washington and Lee, helped me locate some vital data on Zimbabwe while I was visiting.

Arthur Goldsmith (a different one) of the University of Massachusetts at Boston, spent much time and effort on several chapters, giving me detailed comments that were immensely helpful in tying up my loose arguments, particularly in the introduction. Stephen Prince, at the University of Maryland, was extremely helpful in providing high-resolution NASA Landsat photos of Zimbabwe, and giving me more information on land degradation issues facing the country. I am especially indebted to Christopher Mackie, at the National Academy of Sciences, for his numerous insightful comments, probing questions and detailed observations throughout an earlier draft. Kelfala Kallon, at the University of Northern Colorado, served as a reviewer for this book, and gave me a number of thoughtful and relevant criticisms that ultimately made this a far stronger book. I greatly thank him for all the time he spent helping me with this project.

In Winston-Salem, my good friends Wake Clinard and William Blancato helped identify sentence structure problems, spelling mistakes and well as organizational problems. Mark Hall of Wake Forest University gave me valuable suggestions and questions to think about during our workouts at the YMCA. At Salem College, Fran Swajkoski, our department secretary, flawlessly typed up the first draft, and got me going on my way. Errol Clauss in the history department gave excellent suggestions on books covering the British Empire; Richard Johe and Marianne Hayek in the Business and Economics Department also gave useful comments. My good friend and colleague Edward Opoku-Dapaah in the sociology department outlined a number of intriguing questions and suggestions with respect to Zimbabwe's political history. Tsungi Hungwe, a student of mine and a native of Zimbabwe, provided helpful research assistance, and useful comments regarding the culture and history of Zimbabwe. The members of the Faculty Affairs Committee also need to be deeply thanked, in particular Penny Griffin, for believing not only in this project, but also in the virtue of funding yearly sabbaticals. I also thank Dean Eileen Wilson-Oyelaran and President Julianne Thrift for approving the sabbatical. Without a sabbatical, this book could not have been written. The funding of this sabbatical was made possible because of generous gifts to Salem College from Jane Morris Saunier, Dorothy Morris Horn, and Hayden Sanford Sams. They established the Gaither Sisters Endowed Sabbatical, of which I am the first grateful recipient.

My mother, Lucy Richardson, and my siblings, Jan, Pam and David surprised me with a laptop for my birthday two years ago, as an inspiration for working on this book. It not only worked flawlessly, but it saved me countless hours of time, and allowed me to work free of distractions wherever I pleased. With their interest and enthusiasm for the project, I was inspired to work harder than ever. My father, Barrie Richardson, understands economics better than anyone I know, and let me know when jargon was getting in the way of comprehension. His tremendous interest in my research gave me confidence that I had a big story to tell. His comments on various drafts, particularly in the last chapter, were enormously helpful in clarifying arguments. I also thank my three daughters, Madeleine, Anna, and Currin and stepchildren, Devon and Curran, who put up with a dining room table full of books and notes for months on end without complaint.

I also am grateful to my undergraduate economics professors at Kenyon College, namely Professors Richard Trethewey, Paco Bataller, and Bruce Gensemer, for their passion, knowledge and inspiring teaching methods. My doctoral dissertation advisor David Blau at the University of North Carolina also gave me wonderful guidance in the techniques of research.

Lastly, I want to deeply thank my wife Michelle, for her many astute comments and suggestions on the structure of the book as well as the flow and composition of the sentences. Her keen eye for detail helped me make this a book that I hope will be enjoyed by scholars and educated laypersons alike. More importantly, her emotional support was always there when I sometimes felt overwhelmed by the complexity of Zimbabwe's problems; in her loving and supportive way she gave me the confidence, strength and energy to complete this book.

C. J. R.

Department of Economics, Salem College
Winston-Salem, North Carolina
June, 2004

Preface

By Hernando de Soto, President of The Institute for Liberty and Democracy, and author of *The Mystery of Capital.*

What is the key to economic and social progress in developing countries? Why have some countries managed to integrate the vast majority of their population into the official legal system and the market economy, while in many others most people remain mired in poverty, violence, and lack of education? One way to find an answer is by looking at the economic history of those countries that have been able to get ahead. The common denominator turns out to be an inclusive property rights system that provided the necessary underpinnings for the rule of law along with the incentives for sustainable economic growth. If the institution of property rights is not a silver bullet –there is no single solution for development— it is obviously the indispensable ingredient of any solution. At some point in their history, all successful nations established widespread property rights. It happened in the Netherlands and then in England between the seventeenth and nineteenth centuries, and in the United States during the following hundred years. It was also put in place in some of the Asian tiger countries after World War II. Although all these countries now enjoy the status of the first world countries, most were as poor as any third world country is today as recently as four decades ago.

Another approach to the issue of economic development is to analyze what happens when a country with the potential to be developed replaces an incipient property rights system with anarchy. This is the route that Richardson has chosen, by investigating the present crisis in Zimbabwe. Although I have not had the opportunity to work there with my research team from the Institute for Liberty and Democracy, Richardson's results are chilling. During the past decade, life expectancy in Zimbabwe has fallen from 56 years old to 35 – a full 21-year drop. During that same period, agricultural production has plummeted to a third of its previous level; inflation has climbed to almost 600%; foreign investment has virtually vanished; and the government has taken a variety of autocratic measures against the media and political opposition.

That a switch from a system of rights to one of political arbitrariness has failed is not likely to surprise anyone. Without clear rules, it is impossible to begin the massive cooperation and expanded division of labor among citizens to increase their productivity and create prosperity. The irony is that the reforms in Zimbabwe have changed very little in any fundamental way: a system that offered access to property rights over assets to only a privileged elite, while excluding the great majority of citizens, has been replaced by another equally discriminatory system.

Zimbabwe's economic problems, as Richardson points out, are due less to the unsettling fact that the government, gun in hand and in the name of a revolution, has taken the 4,000 most productive agricultural farms of the country away from their owners, and more to the more astonishing fact that a mere 4,000 individuals or families enjoy the benefits of managing the nation's most productive land. A system of accumulation that reserves its advantages and opportunities for only a few people is bound to fail over time. History teaches us that this situation is not unique to Zimbabwe. More than 200 years ago, it was the cause for the French revolution, it continued for centuries more in Russia and China, and it was the situation in Peru and other third world countries not so many decades ago. And their histories teach us that a productive and hard working minority cannot last if the benefits of private property are in the hands of only a few.

What can we do, then, to avoid the repetition of these massive expropriations and the anarchy that ensues? What we know is that a capitalist system with few opportunities for the majority is not democratic capitalism. It is mercantilism –a system of economic rights accessible to so few of its citizens that it cannot provide either the ample base or the solid social contract that makes the concentration of capital acceptable to the majority.

Without widespread participation, space opens up for populist leaders with little imagination for anything but mischief. And without legal property rights for the majority, assets cannot be used to generate capital – i.e., they cannot be used to obtain credit, to attract or obtain investment, or to become liquid so that they can fuel growth. In general, this deprives the great majority of a chance to enjoy a life of greater well being earned through their own efforts.

As Richardson informs us in this extremely important book, arbitrary expropriation does not automatically bring about a more egalitarian economic system. If rights are determined by the supply and demand of oligopolistic rights, the system continues to be mercantilistic and will be as legally and politically unstable as the one that it replaced. People become alienated from it.

Mercantilism is not new. It prevailed in Europe before and during the Industrial Revolution, and, unfortunately, mercantilism continues to be the predominant economic system in most developing countries, even now at the beginning of the twenty-first century. We found it in Peru in the mid-eighties, when my colleagues and I were trying to understand the universal phenomenon of extralegality. And Richardson has made an incredible contribution by finding it in Zimbabwe —land taken from legitimate owners were not, in many instances, given to the poorest, but rather to those who showed unconditional political support for the regime, and to those who had won the personal favor of the government.

The poor in Zimbabwe —like the majority of the poor all over the world— continue to be excluded. In part, this is revealed by the historic exodus of millions of poor Zimbabweans who try to cross the border into one of the neighboring countries, often repeatedly.

Zimbabwe does need a serious revolution. A legal one, and not one that is imposed by force. More specifically, Zimbabwe needs to incorporate into one system widespread legal and extralegal practices, along with customary practices. Such a legal revolution will also spark fundamental economic change if it rest on the aspirations and sense of fairness of the majority. A legal and economic revolution that has confidence in its own people, crafted to help the nation's majority while promoting individual accountability. A revolution that does not benefit a mere 4,000 fortunate and hard working families. Not even Switzerland would remain a democracy and an open market economy if only 4,000 Swiss families had legal property rights.

What is needed in Zimbabwe is the creation of an inclusive, integrated property rights system that not only makes physical possession of assets possible for all citizens but also injects life into assets, thus creating capital. What is required, in other words, is that every parcel of land, every building, every piece of equipment or store of inventories is represented in a property document that is the visible sign of a vast hidden process that connects all these assets to the rest of the economy. Thanks to the representational process that the law creates, assets can lead an invisible, parallel life alongside their material existence. They can be used as collateral for credit. They can also provide a link to the owner's credit history, an accountable address for the collection of debts and taxes, the basis for the creation of reliable and universally available public utilities, and the foundation for the creation of securities that can be rediscounted and sold in secondary markets. This is the process that allows assets to generate capital.

The real alternative to mercantilism (or capitalism for only a few) is not to change the beneficiaries of mercantilism but to make the benefits of property rights accessible to all. In this crucially important book Richardson does the remarkable job of letting us know how badly the ignorance of the role of property rights in development can hurt a nation. Richardson's contribution to the ongoing debate on development is important for all humanity.

Introduction

In 1992, twelve years after Zimbabwe's independence from Great Britain, the future for Zimbabwe looked bright. Agricultural yields were large enough to allow the country to export grain to other countries, a rarity in sub-Saharan Africa. The government offered free education and relatively good access to medical care. Population growth was slowing, and direct foreign investment increasing.

With rich mineral assets, an educated workforce, and beautiful natural wonders, Zimbabwe seemed poised to be an African success story. Economic growth from 1980-89 had averaged a robust 5.2 percent in real terms, and from 1990-1999 it had slowed but still averaged a healthy 2.9 percent. But it was the year 2000 that marked the beginning of the most serious collapse in Zimbabwe's 20-year history. Three years later, Zimbabwe had gone from a place of hope to one of the grimmest places on Earth. Consider these circumstances in 2003:[1]

1. *Life expectancy sharply dropped. Babies born in 1993 could expect to live to 56 years old; ten years later only half would make it to their 35th birthday.*

2. *Real GDP growth collapsed. The economy shrunk by 5 percent in 2000, 8 percent in 2001, 10 percent in 2002 and perhaps as much as 15 percent in 2003.*

3. *Agricultural output dropped to 30 percent of its former level. Half of the population faced starvation in 2004. Zimbabwe used to feed itself and export the rest.*

4. *The money supply increased dramatically, fueling 500% annual inflation.*

5. *Zimbabwean dollars lost more than 99% of their value versus other hard currencies, such as the dollar, since 2000.*

6. *The government's autocratic actions against the media and political opponents earned it the rank of one of the most repressive regimes in the world.*

7. *Direct foreign investment plummeted to nearly zero, as anxious overseas investors transferred their funds to other, less troublesome areas of the globe.*

8. *The International Monetary Fund stripped Zimbabwe of its voting rights in June 2003 after the country failed to make timely payments; it currently owes the Fund $273 million dollars.*

How did an ailing Zimbabwe suddenly fall apart so quickly? Were its markets and institutions like lined-up dominos, with the fall of one leading to the tipping over of the next? Or was Zimbabwe simply a house of cards that collapsed into a chaotic pile?

When I set out to write this book, it was tempting to take the "house of cards" approach. So many problems were happening at once that it seemed an overwhelming task to find the common thread that led to Zimbabwe's quick unraveling, if that thread existed at all. Most articles described a part of the economy, but none knitted them together into a comprehensive explanation. A well-researched 2002 paper from the World Bank titled, "Why Has Poverty Increased In Zimbabwe?" concluded Zimbabwe had gotten poorer because the value of its assets was dropping. But why was the value of its assets falling in the first place? A July 2003 International Monetary Fund report contained a wealth of statistics and laid out the scope of many of Zimbabwe's problems listed above, but again did not provide an underlying answer.[2]

What could account for the crushing speed of this collapse?

In examining dozens of economic indicators, graphs and charts, one thing jumped out. Nearly every economic indicator showed some sort of collapse during or shortly after the year 2000, with Figure A showing the precipitous changes in GDP growth as one example.

There was one significant event that year. President Mugabe's government began the process of seizing thousands of large-scale and white-owned commercial farms during this time, in the name of land reform. Although the government had expropriated farms in the past, the total number was very small, and the owners had been compensated in those cases.

Figure A. Zimbabwe: Changes in GDP Growth, 1981-2003

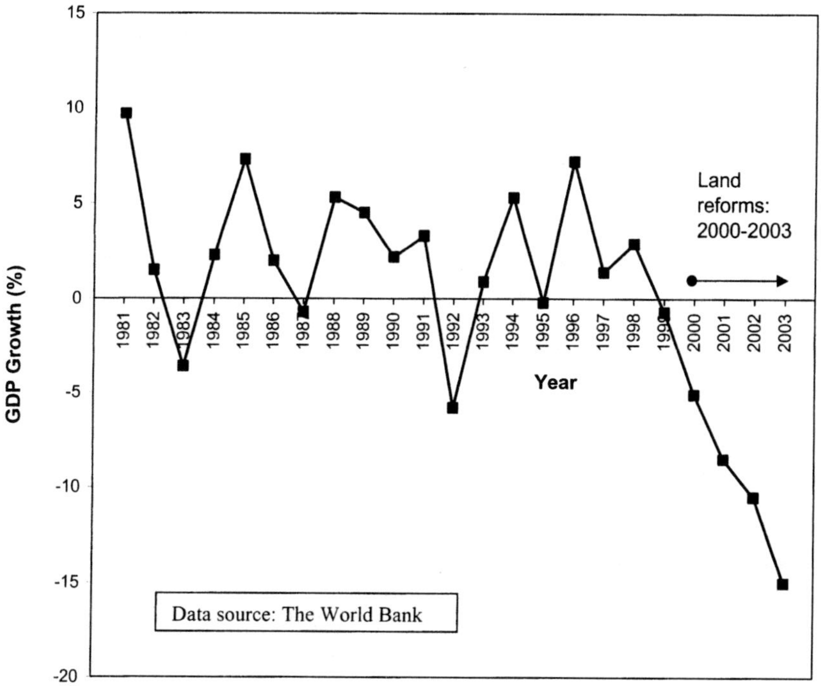

It began on a day in February 2000. That day, the Mugabe government stood idly by, as a group of armed black men forcibly drove a white family off their commercial farm. President Mugabe had long made promises of land reform to address the inequities in land ownership between white and black Zimbabweans, but many black Zimbabweans were growing increasingly impatient. As a result, marauding groups, sometimes backed by veterans of Mugabe's army, grew ever bolder and seized one white-owned commercial farm after another. Over 4,000 farms were ultimately vacated, and dozens of farmers lost their lives. In many cases, the Mugabe government encouraged the takeovers to occur, by listing the targeted farms in the local newspapers as "available."[3] An estimated 350,000 people (nearly all black Zimbabweans) employed by these farms now found themselves unemployed and on the brink of starvation, along with their families and dependents numbering another 1-2 million.[4]

It is certainly true that others have blamed the land seizures for causing a devastating impact. However, the agricultural sector makes up just 15 percent of the economy.[5] How did the seizure of several thousand commercial farms have such a devastating and wide-ranging impact on Zimbabwe's economy? Tourism, manufacturing, mining, and many other industries had made Zimbabwe a veritable economic engine through the 1980s and less so through the 1990s.

The central argument put forth in this book is this: When a government seizes land, it greatly damages the essential linchpin of an economy, and that linchpin is well-secured property rights. As the case of Zimbabwe shows, a market economy is prone to collapse with surprising speed. There are three reasons for this, having to do with land equity, knowledge, and trust.

First, land seizures wiped out billions of dollars worth of land equity- vital for individual borrowing and wealth creation. Newly resettled blacks who were assigned plots of former commercial farmland now have a new property owner- the government. Without land titles, blacks now must lease the land from year to year from the government. With no means to borrow against their land, the new farmers cannot obtain loans from banks for seeds or farm equipment. To illustrate, prior to 1997 Zimbabweans purchased an average of 1,600 tractors per year. In 2002, total countrywide sales had fallen to just eight tractors.[6] The land seizures thus caused a vast constriction of borrowing which rippled from business to business, and sector to sector. Calculations done in this book show that an estimated five billion U.S. dollars in wealth was lost from the agricultural sector in one year, and ultimately more than 75 percent of the entire value of all commercial farmland vanished.[7] This wealth is now locked up in what economist Hernando de Soto has called "dead capital."

Second, the land seizures in Zimbabwe broke a chain of vital business knowledge. By handing off large tracts of productive farmland to inexperienced farmers with no access to capital and little understanding of modern farming methods, yields dropped dramatically in Zimbabwe's once diversified agricultural sector. Maize, groundnuts, cotton, wheat, soybean, sunflowers, coffee and sheep production contracted between 50 and 90 percent during the 2000-2003 period. The contagion then spread to the manufacturing sector, of which 60 percent was directly tied to agricultural output.

Lastly, the land seizures broke down the trust, confidence and perception that the rules of the marketplace would be fairly enforced by the government. The Mugabe government willfully ignored the Zimbabwean law, even after its Supreme Court declared land reforms unconstitutional. Granted, there had been numerous human rights abuses, and wasteful, corrupt expenditures by government officials, but this was far different. An unnerving precedent had been set: For the first time, the executive branch of government condoned the involuntary expropriation of private property, and there was nothing the judicial branch could do. Indeed, President Mugabe simply replaced judges who were not sympathetic toward his aims. Intimidated by these actions, investors and businesspeople worldwide wondered if homes, stocks or other businesses could be next. As a result, direct foreign investment plummeted an astonishing 99 percent in three years, from $443 million in 1998 to about $5 million in 2001. In addition, the World Bank's risk premium on investment in Zimbabwe jumped from 3.4% in 2000 to 20.4% in 2001.[8] For native Zimbabweans, this new lack of legal clarity made it far less attractive to invest time and money for future projects. They too wondered if their other assets were safe.

Certainly, Zimbabwe's collapse was hastened by several other factors. Communal farming methods, used to produce half of Zimbabwe's food, are particularly vulnerable to lack of rainfall and tragedy of the commons, since there are no land titles issued. The lack of land titles in these regions, as well as overcrowding, has led to severe degradation of the land, as shown in the photos in the middle of this book. During the spring of 2002, a drought killed much of the communal lands' crops. Ordinarily the production from commercial farms could have greatly offset the damage, since these farms employ sophisticated irrigation systems. Land seizures thus could not have come at a worse time. However, the underlying issue is that the lack of well-defined property rights caused the collapse of the agricultural sector in 2001. They were wrested away in the commercial lands, and not well defined to begin with in the communal lands.

In addition, many of the nationalized industries were inefficiently run, causing ever-larger deficits for the government. Zimbabwe found itself in a position where its government and economy were totally unequipped for the disastrous ripple effects caused by land seizures. In fact, as we shall see, the government's actions were generally the exact opposite of what should have been done. Instead of finding solutions to the crisis, it became increasingly inflexible. The government used more and more of its resources to vainly control prices, exchange rates and black market activities, while printing money ever faster. Moreover, it seized profits from gold mines, leading to nationwide shutdowns. Thus, the land seizures were the first domino in a chain of events that spread out much further than the agricultural sector; they affected nearly every aspect of society.

The land reform movement in Zimbabwe serves as a tragic natural experiment, illustrating the strengths and weaknesses of any market-based economy. Markets can endure distortions, subsidies, and price controls, showing remarkable resiliency. Zimbabwe's agricultural sector has always been heavily regulated, and these regulations have led to wasteful government spending, lower productivity, and other inefficiencies. In spite of this, Zimbabwe was once one of the most productive agricultural producers in Africa. The regulations, while less than ideal from an economic point of view, were at least enforced with consistency. The economic damage done by them was limited because people still had confidence that they would profit and retain the fruits of their labor.

It is when property rights are damaged that an economy exhibits great fragility. When the fruits of labor are at risk, this strikes at the heart of all economic activity. The fragility increases exponentially as the economy develops and becomes more interconnected domestically and globally. There is more to lose for more people, and it happens more quickly. The focus of this book is to argue this central point, using the case of Zimbabwe as a most compelling example. By examining the state of its economy in close detail before and after the land seizures, this book hopes to show how property rights are the vital and disarmingly simple connecting piece that holds a vastly complex economy together. The case of Zimbabwe illustrates that property rights are an economy's linchpin, which once broken, can bring an economy to its knees.

In spite of the gloomy analysis regarding the consequences of land reform, this book aims to be more than a depressing chronicle of how not to run a country. Halfway around the globe, Nicaragua experienced much the same devastation as Zimbabwe after its own land reform movement in the early 1980s- hyperinflation, crashing GDP growth, and a tremendous decline in wealth. Yet within five years after the election of a moderate government, Nicaragua's economy began to bloom again from the midst of the rubble. Despite two years of pro-market policies, its economic recovery occurred only after the government began a concerted effort to restore property titles to their rightful owners.

The book proceeds in the following way. The primary task of Chapter 1 is to demonstrate why property rights are a free market's crucial linchpin. It does this by first giving a brief historical overview of the concurrent evolution of property rights and markets. It then reviews the property rights literature, primarily in the field of economics. After that, it delves more deeply into the key theoretical and practical importance of property rights in the marketplace, by integrating distinct ideas from Adam Smith, Hernando de Soto and others into a more comprehensive picture. The picture helps us understand how a simple mechanism for ownership can underpin a vast network of wealth in a country.

Chapter 2 shows how the political evolution of property rights and government laws came to its present-day form in Zimbabwe. This is done by first analyzing how Zimbabwe's own cultural past, rooted in its tribal identities, led to wholly different notions about the nature of property rights than in the Western world. The colonial exploits of the British created a tension between these different viewpoints, which ultimately shaped and influenced the state of affairs in Zimbabwe today. In addition, this chapter evaluates Zimbabwe's structure of government, in order to show its past experience with democracy and legislation of property rights, as well as its prospects for encouraging future economic growth.

Chapter 3 delves into the all-important agricultural sector, with an eye towards understanding its history and tensions caused by land reform. It then explores the ramifications of property conflicts within the communal lands, caused by the clashing interests of the village chiefs and the local government bodies. Differences in land ownership and production between white and black commercial farmers are also laid out, illustrating the (misguided) political rationale for land reform. Lastly, the politically sensitive issue of water rights is recounted, putting Zimbabwe's quest for water in the context of its neighboring countries, as well as its own property rights.

While Chapter 3's goal is to describe the agriculture sector's history, structure and conflicts, Chapter 4 analyzes in detail the seeds and outcome of its collapse. It first shows the damaging effects of government price controls, which resulted in chronic deficits and distortions in market signals. Next, this chapter evaluates the effectiveness of the World Bank-imposed economic reforms. In addition, this chapter challenges the common belief that a severe drought was one of the central factors causing the collapse of the agricultural sector, using rainfall data from Zimbabwe's Department of Meteorology. Although communal farmers were certainly devastated, the loss in wealth caused by the collapse of the commercial agricultural sector's property values had far more damaging long-term consequences.

As the agricultural sector collapsed, the manufacturing and banking sectors soon followed. The global financial network now followed suit, with most investors selling off Zimbabwean dollars. Chapter 5 chronicles the resulting free fall of Zimbabwe's currency, as well as the spillover effects. The chapter also contrasts the effects of two different economic policies in the mining sector. Those differences led to gold mines shutting down on the one hand, while platinum mining boomed. Also seen in this chapter is how the central bank of Zimbabwe exacerbated the situation through excessive money supply growth.

With a failing domestic currency and increased difficulty in paying for imports, Zimbabwe's once vaunted education and health care system took an enormous shock. Chapter 6 describes the background and history of these two institutions, and then relates their subsequent decline after the year 2000. It also describes the changes in population growth rates as a result of the AIDS epidemic.

Chapter 7 gives background on the labor market, and how it reacted to the economic collapse, putting focus on the importance of the formal and informal sector. Women play a vital role in the labor market and this is also explored. The latter part of the chapter focuses on women's rights and status in society, their economic role in the family, and how this has all changed more recently in light of the economic collapse. (Figure B on the next page gives an overview of Zimbabwe's collapse in a schematic form.)

Chapter 8, the concluding chapter, strives to end on a positive note. Using a comparison case of Nicaragua, there is evidence that a country can indeed climb out of a tremendous mess with some simple but far-reaching changes. Those changes, not surprisingly, include the rebuilding of basic property rights as a first step. Thus, it is hoped that readers of this book come away with a greater appreciation for property rights' invisible yet essential function for every free-market economy around the world.

Figure B. Zimbabwe: Anatomy of a Collapse

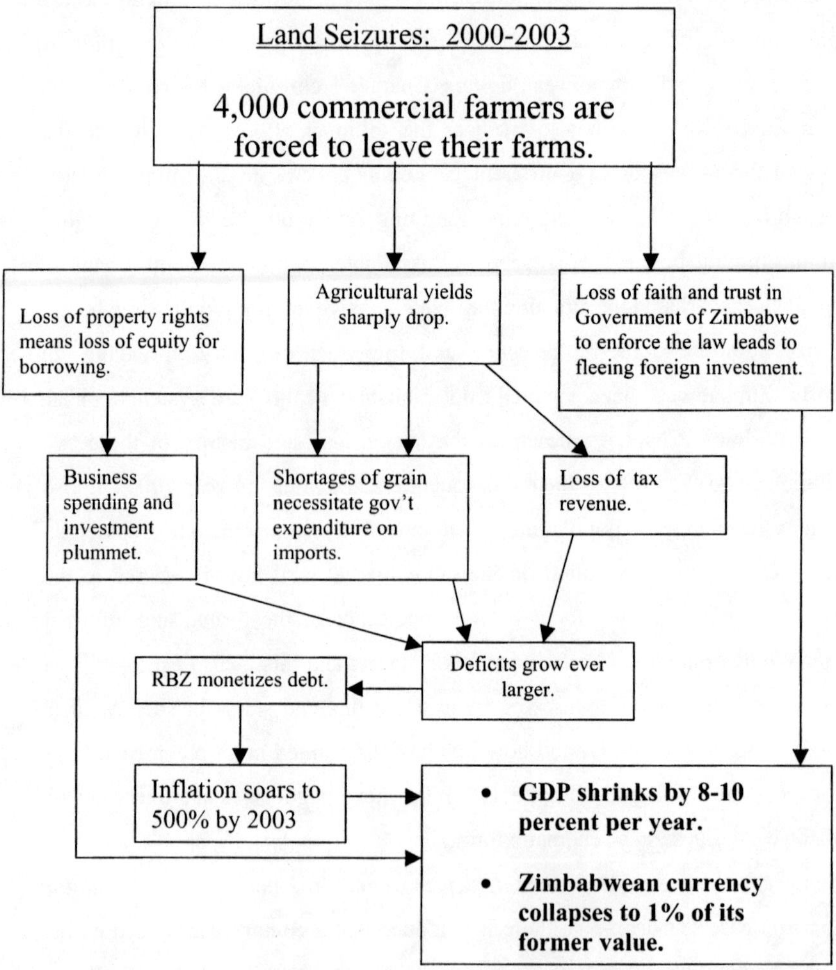

Resulting impact of land seizures:

- A law against hoarding cash goes into effect.
- Half the country faces starvation.
- Direct foreign investment shrivels up.
- GDP declines 5-10% each year.
- AIDS cases rapidly increase.
- Professional work force emigrates.
- Queues for basic foodstuffs increases.
- Black markets emerge for gasoline, hard currency.
- RBZ prints currency ever faster.
- Political freedoms are repressed.
- Unemployment grows to 70%.

Chapter 1. The Critical Importance of Property Rights

A Short History

If one opens up a typical introductory economics textbook, the relationship between property rights and economic growth is generally consigned to a small section; sometimes it is not mentioned at all. This is reflected by the passing attention it receives in the economic literature. Property rights serve as the linchpin for markets, but because they quietly work so well behind the scenes of the industrialized world, they are generally taken for granted.

It wasn't always this way. Countries that first recognized the importance of property rights were the ones that saw the fastest economic growth. In particular, England has a very long history in this regard. In 1086, William the Conqueror sent out his commissioners to exhaustively record every piece of property in England, putting these records in the so-called Domesday Book. By doing so, it made legitimate all the changes in land ownership since the conquest.[1] In 1580, Queen Elizabeth I authorized Francis Drake's extraordinarily risky voyage around the world in the Golden Hind. Drake got to keep (in modern day terms) millions of dollars from the spoils of his journey. His shipmates were amply rewarded as well.[2] By doing so, Queen Elizabeth I conveyed a message to all of her English citizens: One has a right to keep the property one has earned, and moreover, extraordinary risks shall be compensated by extraordinary rewards.

As the growth of markets enriched European merchants in the 18th centuries, the business class successfully pressured their governments to create policies that protected their property from encroachment by monarchs and lords. Prior to that, monarchs and lords could take a merchant's possessions at will, necessitating a large number of secret transactions that naturally slowed the flow of commerce.[3]

Another important innovation during this time was the legal enforcement of contracts. Contracts protected an individual's private property, by ensuring to each individual that the asset given up would be met with another asset, presumably of greater worth to each individual. As Goldsmith (1995) points out, contracts do two things: First, they allow exchanges of assets to take place at different points in time. An order of cabbage paid for today can be delivered tomorrow. Second, contracts allow people to trade with strangers. They increase the confidence of individuals to do more business, and more importantly, vastly increase the level of possibilities for transactions, including the offering of labor services. With every step taken along this legal path, the benefits to hard work, risk and investment increased for private individuals.

One of the primary ways that England established itself as the world's wealthiest empire was by essentially exporting its legal system of property rights to other countries. England's primary tack in gaining footholds in other countries was shrewd in many respects. Rather than investing the resources in moving navies and armies to various parts of the globe, it instead gave free rein to an explorer/entrepreneur (or a rapacious colonist, depending on one's point of view). In exchange for the right to charter laws and regulations, England allowed the explorer to keep most of the gains from his venture. So for example, when Cecil Rhodes founded the British South Africa Company in 1889, he was allowed to exploit and profit from tapping into Zimbabwe's rich natural resources (not unlike Francis Drake, centuries before). Other countries, particularly the Netherlands, Spain and France followed this model as well, carving up Africa into separate colonies. It is important to emphasize, however, that these explorers paid little attention to the informal and highly localized systems of land ownership employed by the native populations. They simply expropriated land as their own, using superior firepower to kill those who opposed the takeover.

It should be noted that the land seizures by the colonialists did not cause immediate economic collapse because the economies in Africa were for the most part undeveloped. There was simply not far for them to fall. However, the seizure of wealth is never conducive to long-term economic growth, because it simply redistributes a stock of assets from one party to another. A superior system must replace the former one in order for the rate of economic growth to improve. The English created the ingredients necessary for a market system to thrive, crucially based on a version of government-defended property rights that were upheld through legal enforcement of contracts and property titles. As we shall see later on, this system was constructed to unabashedly help the English settlers many times more than the native Africans. Economic growth occurred because within the new economic system the rules and regulations were consistently enforced, at least among the English, which ultimately benefited the economy at large. However, the initial seizures and the vast income differentials did establish a long-running tension between the two populations, setting the stage for the ultimate collapse of Zimbabwe in the year 2000.

With regard to Britain's other former colonies, a 1998 survey indicated that these countries now include some of the healthiest economies today. They include: The United States, Singapore, Hong Kong, Thailand and Ireland.[4] Those countries had the strongest legal protection of investors, including both shareholders and creditors. Well-defended legal protection translates into more security and less risk for investors. With that comes much higher rates of capital formation.

The United States did not initially have a smooth transition, however, because England gave more free rein to the United States than other countries. At the beginning of the 19th century, its property rights laws were still in utter chaos. Confusing laws abounded, encouraging squatters to take parcels of land, causing conflict with legal authorities and Native Americans. Congress opposed giving squatters titles for many years, despite hundreds of thousands of settlers occupying public land. After an exhausting and serpentine route, property rights in the United States eventually became uniform, formalized and secure.[5] Yet their importance is buried in the past and economists, like most people, place more attention on things that change.

Literature Review on Property Rights and Economic Growth

In the economics literature, most of the relatively recent work explaining economic growth has been framed by neo-classical models that underscore investment in technology, human capital and international trade flows (Solow, 1956; Romer, 1986; Grossman and Helpman, 1991). These models offer important insights into causes of economic growth, but they implicitly assume that there are well-enforced private property rights.[6] This assumption is not valid for many lesser-developed countries. The danger is that if property rights are taken for granted then an essential piece of the puzzle is left out when making policy prescriptions. The first question ought to be "How well established is this country's property rights?"

Sociologists also neglect this importance of property rights in shaping markets, as pointed out by Campbell and Lindberg (1990). They note that only "a handful" of scholars pays more than "sporadic" attention to this issue; most focus more attention on criticizing the market outcomes as a result of property rights rather than understanding how property rights fundamentally shape markets. One notable exception is Block (1986), who notes that a useful metaphor is to think of property rights and the economy as connected by a "membrane" that permits constant interaction between the legal and economic systems. Another is Granovetter (1985), who argues that we must understand how such institutions are fully embedded in society in order to know how to improve economic performance.[7]

To be sure, there is a relatively small group of economists who have cast their eyes toward this important subject, going all the way back to Adam Smith in 1776 and much later, Frank Knight (1971). Both saw property rights as a key ingredient in markets, because it secured the value of one's work effort. Economic historians such as North (1973) and Rosenberg (1994) have argued that property rights are important with respect to long-run economic growth. Scully (1988) provided empirical evidence of this, reporting that countries with well-developed property rights and market structures experienced, on average, 2.6% GDP growth, compared to 1.1% in countries where property rights were limited and there was a great deal of state intervention. Torstensson (1994) found that in a country-by-country comparison, arbitrary seizures of property decelerate economic growth. His study predicted that a country might increase its growth rate by more than one percentage point by putting a stop to such seizures. Of the fifteen countries in his study that undertook arbitrary seizure of property, nine had negative growth rates. They included Chad (-6.1%), Liberia (-4.0%) and Zaire (-5.1%). Those findings appear to underestimate the total impact of property seizures, at least in the case of Zimbabwe. Goldsmith (1995) concluded that second and third world countries enjoyed faster growth when they had more secure property rights, as measured by a Heritage Foundation index.

Since the empirical studies were cross-sectional they can only address the issue of whether or not property rights influence economic growth. The studies all agree that they do. Yet what this book aims to do is to provide a compelling example of just how quickly an economy can crash once its property rights are damaged. To begin this journey, it is first necessary to delve more deeply into the ways property rights provide the crucial incentives for economic growth. By doing so, one can better understand how they serve as the crucial underpinning for any developing market economy.

The Link Between Property Rights and Growth

Property rights actually spawn two separate pathways that are both important in fueling economic growth. The first pathway is the dramatic effect on work incentives when individuals feel secure that the product of their work efforts will not be stolen from them. The second pathway is the potential created by allowing someone to transform property into a liquid asset through a secured loan on that property. This *vastly* multiplies opportunities for entrepreneurial activity. When enforced by the state, both pathways create a type of an insurance mechanism that safeguards against loss. The first one safeguards individuals, the second safeguards lenders. Both pathways create incentives for a country's citizens to work harder, and take more risks. This is a case when moral hazard* may be a desired outcome of such an "insurance policy". Understanding the impact of each one is vitally important to understanding Zimbabwe's collapse, as both pathways were blocked through the misguided actions of its government.

Pathway one: Securing the fruits of one's labor

First and foremost, property rights help secure for individuals the fruits of their labor. Adam Smith made this point when he wrote: "Commerce and manufactures can seldom flourish long in any state which does not enjoy a regular administration of justice, in which people do not feel themselves secure in possession of their property, in which the faith of contracts is not supported by the law..." (1937:862). Frank Knight went further, declaring property rights the "essential ingredient for economic progress."[8] In his classic 1971 work, *Risk, Uncertainty and Profit*, he says:

> Let us begin with the relation of capital in the sense of material goods to the fundamental structure of society. The facts of progress will be seen to have an intimate connection with the very institution of private property. In an unprogressive society private property in the modern sense of the term need not exist. The social justification of private ownership is that the coupling of control of resources with enjoyment of the fruits of their use is supposed to give an incentive to use the goods effectively in production. [9]

---

* Moral hazard is defined as the increase in risky behavior that may occur once one is insured. For example, people with theft insurance are less likely to lock up.

When people do not feel secure, they try to insure against losses. Where governments have responded with well-secured property rights laws, this has resulted in the creation of a public good. The government protects against losses due to trespassers, potential squatters, or other criminal activity. Private insurance markets fill in the rest of the potential losses from such things as fire, floods and the like. All of these things increase the work initiative and productivity of the property owners. This of course vastly increases economic output. There is new evidence of this in the case of Peru, where the nationwide effort to secure land titles has vastly increased the labor supply. According to preliminary research, Peruvians have entered the work force in far greater numbers instead of spending time guarding their property.[10]

Of course, the opposite happens when property rights become increasingly ill-defined. As we shall see in greater detail in Chapter 2, Zimbabweans living in so-called communal lands have informal and often muddy rules about procedures relating to land transfers, use, and ownership rights. Rarely is there a simple and secure transaction between two assets, money and land. More often, the will of the chief and the preferences of the other villagers play an important role in who gets what land. Complicating matters, the socialist aims of the Mugabe government have resulted in top-down policies that seek to reallocate land into egalitarian plots, regardless of villagers' past investment in them. Predictably, this has led to frustration and less willingness to work and take care of the land.

Pathway two: Borrowing for the future

The second role property rights play is that they allow individuals to borrow against their property for consumption and investment purposes. In effect, they allow property owners to transform a highly illiquid asset such as a house into a highly liquid one (cash), using a secured loan. At the same time, property rights lower the risk to lenders, by coupling the property's deed with the loan. This vastly lowers potential losses for banks. Loans increase as a result, as does economic activity.

Hernando de Soto's elegantly argued *Mystery of Capital* (2000) underscores this generally missed, but key point. His question, "Why does capitalism triumph in certain countries and fail everywhere else?" is answered by closely examining well-defined property rights systems that distinguish successful yet culturally diverse economies, from Japan to Germany to the United States. Surprisingly, he points out that the world's poor living outside the West have far more wealth than we have previously imagined. Much of the wealth is tied up in their homes, as it is in the West. As an example, Haiti has 158 times more wealth in property than in all the foreign aid received up to 1995.[11] The difference is that property rights are not well defined in lesser-developed countries, or are extremely difficult to acquire. Legally acquiring land in Haiti takes nineteen years, and 176 bureaucratic steps.[12] In Egypt it can take between 6-14 years to gain access to land for construction purposes. It is no surprise then, that the majority of people in lesser-developed countries have no legal title to their land or property.

What we take for granted, de Soto argues, is how the simplification of property rights created a tremendous potential for economic growth in the United States and other Western countries. By having a title to the land, owners of property can transform equity in their house into startup funds for a new business, or remodeling their home. These funds are then funneled to other individuals, who can in turn invest in their own entrepreneurial projects. This is a type of a multiplier effect: Property transforms from a locked-up asset into a malleable form of liquid wealth connected across a string of individuals. In de Soto's words, "dead capital" has been transformed into "living capital". Not only that, but having an address makes the homeowner accountable to creditors, reducing the creditor's prospect of financial loss.

De Soto writes, "A property system creates a *network* (italics mine) through which people can assemble their assets into more valuable combinations."[13] Indeed, the U.S. economic slowdown of 2001-2003 was ameliorated to a large extent because of the millions of Americans who took advantage of historically low interest rates, and refinanced their homes, freeing up cash to be spent elsewhere. Without well-defined property rights that we take for granted, our economy could have plunged into a much deeper and longer recession.

In his book, de Soto demonstrates how millions of dollars of wealth have been created in Peru since he and his colleagues at the Institute for Liberty and Democracy worked with the government to simplify Peru's property rights structure. He underscores how long it can take to build confidence in a country's legal system (it took over two years of public debate in Peru to pass reform laws aimed at simplifying the process for obtaining property titles).

What de Soto and others have not yet examined is how quickly this multiplier effect collapses when things go in reverse. Land titles serve as a bridge towards opening up pathways and networks of economic activity; unfortunately, because they are an integral yet invisible component, this makes an economic system vulnerable to quick economic collapse. Understanding the ramifications of the commercial farm sector of Zimbabwe fits well with the second pathway, as the ripple effects spilled across financial sectors with surprising speed. Through this prism, this story is explored in far more detail in Chapter 4.

Other Evidence[a]

The World Bank (1999) sees land titling as "an essential step to provide security of tenure and incentives to extend rural financial services to small-scale farming families."[14] Research has shown that investments in land improvements on titled land were 1.4-2.2 times higher than on untitled land in Paraguay, Thailand, Brazil and Honduras (Alson, 1996; Feder, 1999). Land security also encourages conservation and sustainable use of natural resources, as shown by Heltberg (2002). In Central America, deforestation and environmental degradation have brought renewed attention to land titling and the security of property rights (Lutz, 1998; Utting, 1996). There is also evidence from Thailand (Feder et al.,1988) and Honduras (Feder, 1999) that shows the positive improvement in credit access and land prices after issuing formal land titles. Titled farms obtained 3-4 times as

[a] Much of this evidence is reported in a fine literature review done by Broegaard et.al. (2002).

much credit as untitled farms. Furthermore, titled land was valued 1.8 times higher than untitled land in both countries.

In order for land titling to improve investment incentives, land markets, and the credit supply, the government must properly enforce property rights. Broegaard, et.al. (2002) report that in Nicaragua, formal land documents are preferred over informal land tenure arrangements. This is because they increase the value of the land by giving better incentives to invest and engage in long-term land use, such as growing perennial crops. All of this results in higher output. They also noted that rural credit markets need to be developed in tandem, as titling currently has little impact on the credit supply in Nicaragua. They conclude that without formal titles, landowners in Nicaragua tend to be rich individuals with liquid assets, who are not necessarily the most productive users of the land.

How Modulating Property Rights Affects the Value of Land.

As we have seen, well-secured property rights increase the incentives to work, and make it a far safer venture for banks to issue loans. When those rights are secured, there is tremendous potential for increased economic growth.

There is a third factor to think about as well. With property rights usually come responsibilities and limits on the use of the land. These limits, such as forbidding the dumping of contaminants that taint the water supply, may be in the best interest of the community. Industrialized countries use zoning laws and environmental regulations to limit those negative spillover effects, or "negative externalities." However, in lesser-developed countries, where land values are low to begin with, it can be argued that limits on land use generally do more harm than good. For this reason, as use regulations decrease in lesser-developed countries, the land's value generally rises, which translates into more equity and greater potential for loans and economic growth.

In Zimbabwe, it can be argued that the hodgepodge of use restrictions plays a far larger role in devaluing the property, along with the lack of formal titling, than externalities ever would. The following framework describes how these use restrictions may ratchet up or down the value of property.[15]

a. Comprehensiveness

This refers to the number and types of resources that the household can control on his or her property. For example, a household might have jurisdiction over the farmland, but not the mineral rights to the land. In each case, the higher the comprehensiveness, the more the land is worth.

b. Exclusiveness

This refers to the ability to keep other households from using and/or exploiting the land, as free riders. A privately owned lake means the public is prevented from gaining access, and possibly polluting its waters without paying for the cleanup. A public meadow will not be tended as a privately owned one would, and if there are grazing animals, the meadow will likely be overgrazed. Property rights that are not well defined generally lead to under-investment in that resource, since the potential investor only gets a share of the return, while everyone else enjoying the property gets the benefits for free. This is usually quite irksome to the property holder. Thus, the greater the exclusiveness, the more the land is worth.

c. Use designation

In modern cities, zones are a way of controlling the spread of economic activity in well-defined and orderly ways. Retail enterprises are sometimes restricted to certain zones, and industrial factories to another. In a less developed region, land may be designated for different types of agricultural uses, such as growing grain, or growing trees. This limits an individual's entrepreneurial activities, and potential income. Although these use designations can bring about an improvement in the overall design and use of the village, town or city, on an individual basis these use designations likely lower the net value of the property at this stage of development.

d. Limits on size

In some cases, the government parcels out the size of the land. If a businessperson cannot buy adjoining land by law, and his or her business is increasing in size, then labor will be the only input that can increase. That will inevitably lead to slower growth due to the law of diminishing returns. An example is a farmer who would like to invest in modern mechanical harvesting equipment, but cannot make it pay with a small plot of land. Economies of scale are only realized as the land gets larger in size. This increases the value of the land.

e. Transferability

The ability of a property owner to sell or give his land away is one of the most important criteria affecting the value of the land. When property is freely transferable, it allows resources to move to their most productive uses; from lower valued uses to more highly valued ones. When those transactions are limited, to say, certain individuals in a village, then that will sharply decrease the value of the property. The reason for this is that those particular individuals may not value the land as highly as another outsider would. An outsider may wish to develop the land, whereas a villager may be content to keep the land as, for instance, a meadow.

f. Security

Property owners place value on property based on their perception that their investment will be protected against loss. When there are a large number of incidents involving land disputes, or the government usurps land without compensation, then property owners feel insecure about the future, and are less likely to invest or upgrade their property. If property insurance is unavailable, then this too will also lower security. The exception to this is the case where squatters on unclaimed land invest in land development in order to strengthen their property claims.[16]

* * * * *

Prior to 2000, Zimbabwe's most economically productive sectors were those with well-defined property rights, in particular, the commercial farms, manufacturing firms and mining sectors. These sectors leveraged their equity to obtain capital such as machinery and tools. Work initiative was high, and individuals were rewarded with profits and stable jobs. These sectors employed well over 1 million people. The mining and manufacturing sectors are now collapsing, and what remains after the land seizures are the communal farm areas, which by and large lack property titles, and also have a bewildering array of limits on use.

With no equity, and no ownership, work initiative is vastly lower than on commercial farms. (Villagers working on lower quality farmland make this worse.) Yet villagers accept many of the regulations because of other benefits that they confer, as will be explored in Chapter 3. These benefits, along with the sense among many that the system of white commercial farms created great economic inequities and was morally unjust, made it politically popular to scrap agricultural land titles. Although the benefits may have appeared obvious, the costs of seizing farmland were far more hidden, and larger than almost everyone could have guessed.

Summary

We have seen the three ways that property rights promote worker productivity. Adam Smith and others after him emphasize the improvement in work initiative. Hernando de Soto reminds us of how land titles allow people to leverage their illiquid property into a liquid asset, creating a network of wealth throughout the economy. Finally, a property's inherent worth can be dramatically manipulated by the state through a number of laws and regulations, which also influences the ultimate size of the network of wealth. (Figure 1.1 below gives an overview of these concepts.) All of these factors play an enormously significant role in determining both the level of a country's wealth and its economic growth.

Importantly, this book does not suggest that secure property rights are the general cure-all for a country's problems. They are a necessary but not sufficient pre-condition for economic growth. Other important factors include free and open markets, access to resources, a law-abiding population and a government not susceptible to corruption. However, the central point of this book is to suggest that secure property rights are the key linchpin to a developing market economy. When property rights are heavily damaged, as in the case of land seizures, an economy can fall apart very quickly, as shown in dramatic fashion by Zimbabwe. In addition, without a government defending and securing property rights, any country will find it very difficult to thrive economically over the long term.

Figure 1.1. The Relationship between Property Rights and GDP growth.

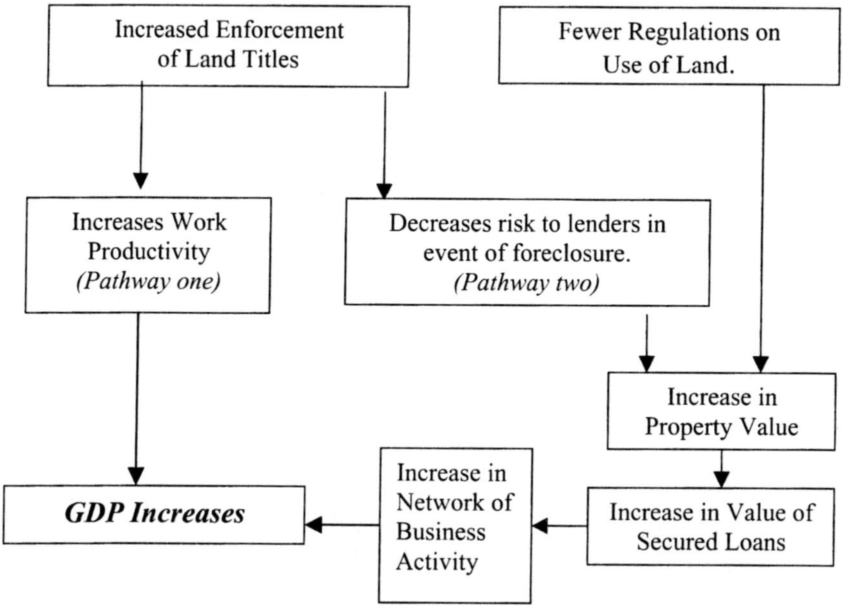

Chapter 2. Zimbabwe's History and Government Protection of Property Rights

History of Property Rights in Zimbabwe

The origin of Zimbabwe's current property rights evolved from the interactions of the two largest tribes, the Shona and the Ndebele (who collectively make up about 95% of Zimbabwe's population) and the white European population. Both of these tribes coexisted prior to the arrival of Europeans in the late 1800s, but on somewhat uneasy terms. The Shona primarily concentrated on farming in the plateau region, while the more free-roaming Ndebele raised livestock. The Ndebele tribe had larger goals than coexistence, however, and through the 1800s the Ndebele tribe either conquered or asked for the Shona to voluntarily give up their land. By the 1850s, the Ndebele state emerged, with a more formal governing structure, and began conscripting men into regiments, on a town-by-town basis. Periodically these regiments would seek to incorporate other towns, sometimes forcibly. The Ndebele men stole the Shona's precious cattle, and sometimes kidnapped and mistreated Shona women.

In the 1860s tales from explorers and missionaries began trickling into Europe about supposed lodes of gold found in the surrounding region. It was impossible to stop the Europeans' entry. As they entered, they petitioned the Ndebele leader, Lobengula, for exploration rights in areas where the Shona lived. Either Lobengula pretended to have influence over the Shona, or the Europeans assumed it; either way there was little to be lost from Lobengula's perspective. But the

Europeans pressed for more. In 1888, Lobengula signed the infamous Rudd Concession, which granted Rhodes' British South Africa Company (BSAC) the rights to "all metals and minerals situated and contained in my kingdom...together with full power to do all things necessary to win and procure the same."[17] Some have seen him as a sellout, although he may have had little choice, when faced with the Europeans' firepower. It has also been argued that Lobengula did not know what he was signing, not being literate in English. In any event, the dispersal of the wealth didn't stop there. A year later, Lobengula signed a charter with Rhodes' BSAC that allowed Rhodes to enter treaties, create laws and a police force, and undertake public works in what would become Southern Rhodesia.[18]

Rhodes' perspective was evidenced by the following quote: "...although we had a charter we had not got the country, which was occupied by savages."[19] Rhodes, the treasure hunter, was now keenly interested in finding the gold. He recruited an armed group of several hundred prospector-adventurers to send into the bush, and in Rhode's words, "began the first groundwork of making a country."[20] Disappointingly, little gold was found, and facing large losses, Rhodes looked to South Africa's DeBeers to make a deal. DeBeers agreed to bail out Rhodes, in exchange for a massive amount of land in Southern Rhodesia, nearly a quarter of a million hectares. (A hectare is equal to 2.47 acres.) Despite the failure to find gold, Rhodes didn't stop promoting Rhodesia, falsely reporting "everywhere new finds are occurring daily."[21]

Rhodes' ambitions didn't stop there. In 1893 the theft of telegraph wire near Fort Victoria gave Rhodes the excuse he was looking for. He declared war against Lobengula, and with a small force of armed men and powerful rapid-fire Maxim guns, quickly overwhelmed the leaders of the Ndebele state. A humiliated Lobengula went into exile, having first sold the land underneath his people, and now having lost the land itself.

Property rights were ignored in other areas as well. The Europeans stole most of the Ndebele's 200,000 cattle, which were the native Zimbabweans' primary source of wealth. By 1897 only 14,000 cattle remained in the hands of the Ndebele- Rhodes and his followers had now stripped them of their lands and their most prized possessions. However, angry uprisings by the native population against Rhodes began costing him millions of pounds. He needed a new source of income, and came up with a plan. He would build a railroad that would enable streams of laborers to reach new gold mines that had been found to be productive.

The plan worked for Rhodes. Whites and blacks from surrounding areas filled the trains, and settled in Rhodesia. Following the miners came farmers, and by 1914 there were around two thousand white farmers growing 74,000 hectares of maize and tobacco. The growing wealth of Southern Rhodesia changed its image; the British now saw it as a hospitable and leisurely retreat. Meanwhile, many black Rhodesians struggled to make ends meet, having lost their valuable farmland and cattle.

Rhodes was finding gold now in greater quantities, but unfortunately the large-scale mines stripped away some of the most productive farmland. This led to over-farming on much of the remaining land, along with erosion and loss of soil nutrients. Tensions increased between the Shona and Ndebele tribes, in light of increasing competition for land resources.[22]

In 1923, white Rhodesians elected to change the status to a "self-governing" colony, and held elections to determine Parliament members. Through the following years, the black population continued to exert pressure on the whites, in an attempt to gain more political power. The small minority of whites now controlled major manufacturing interests, and the manufacturing base was booming. From 1953 to 1957 the Southern Rhodesian manufacturing sector increased from 700 to 1300 firms.[23] Typically these firms, from farming operations to mines, wanted low-cost labor that could be drawn from the native population. Rights of these laborers were little to none; for example, no worker could strike unless he or she had sought to handle the case through all other grievance mechanisms. The government in the late 1950s debated giving universal voting privileges, but rejected it on the grounds that whites' fate would be entirely in the hands of the black majority. Instead, the government assembly allowed blacks to vote if they made a yearly income of $672 and a satisfactory performance on a literacy test. In practice, the vast majority of blacks made much less than that. The other way blacks could vote was if they completed a grammar school education. Yet just in case either of these two avenues proved "too successful", the whites stacked the deck in another way: Once the number of blacks reached twenty percent of the white voting population, no more would be allowed to vote. In other words, about 12,000 blacks could vote, even thought there were 50,000 black voters eligible, and several million blacks of voting age in the general population.[24] Despite this, educated blacks generally saw this as a step forward from no voting rights at all.

Voting rights did little to assuage the frustration of ordinary Zimbabwean citizens. The highest paid wages in "Grade A" were nearly all earned by whites, and workers in this grade earned nine times more than in "Grade B". Black commercial farm workers were paid such low wages, for example, that 90 percent of their children were malnourished.[25] Blacks became increasingly agitated about the inequitable "partnership" lauded by the government. Pressure was growing for something to happen, and whites began fearing what might happen if racial tensions erupted into violence.

By 1962, Britain was pushing for majority rule, and offered independence for Rhodesia as an incentive. However, conservative white Rhodesians dug in their heels and felt threatened by the thought of majority rule. From their colonialist perspective, their entire way of life could be lost. Conservative whites were not about to give in if they could help it.

Ian Douglas Smith, a native born Rhodesian and a member of the Rhodesian Front (RF), became prime minister in 1964, and fit the bill for the conservative agenda with his renegade attitude. Rather than embrace majority rule and "one man- one vote", the Smith and the RF took a risky gambit by completely steering their country in the opposite direction. Facing worldwide ostracism, the Rhodesian Front made a Unilateral Declaration of Independence (UDI) in 1965, in effect formally disconnecting themselves from any sort of influence from the United Kingdom. The British reacted by punishing Rhodesia using every economic tool at their disposal. They de-linked Rhodesia's currency from the English pound, banned its capital exports, seized the Rhodesian Reserve Bank's assets in London, boycotted Rhodesian tobacco exports, and suspended the country from the Commonwealth.[26]

The Smith government retaliated by defaulting on their loans to Britain, as well as World Bank loans backed by Britain. The UK and much of the rest of the world responded with international sanctions in 1967, although some countries such as South Africa openly ignored them.

Almost no one predicted Smith's regime would last. With barely 220,000 whites holding political power in a country of more than 5,000,000 blacks, most observers predicted an immediate downfall. But Smith had important factors that helped him achieve a lock on political power, including an efficient and loyal army (which included enlisted blacks), help from South Africa, and far superior firepower. Most importantly, white Rhodesians across almost all age groups and classes enthusiastically helped fight the burgeoning guerilla resistance. There was even a division with 51-60 year old men.[27]

Economically, Rhodesia did surprisingly well in the face of these sanctions. The United States was doing business with Rhodesia by 1972, buying chrome, and the manufacturing base increased from 19 percent of GDP in 1965 to 24 percent in 1975. The economic success came about because of Smith's effort to thwart the isolation from the rest of the world. Smith's government forced foreign firms on Rhodesian soil to keep their profits within the borders, and these companies could not import essential materials without the consent of the government. Education for blacks and wage increases were also cut in order to stave off budget shortfalls.

From 1966 to 1979, the guerilla attacks became increasingly aggressive, as black militant organizations grew more organized. The Zimbabwe African People's Union (ZAPU), whose members were largely from the Ndebele tribe, and the Zimbabwe African National Union (ZANU) from the Shona tribe, operated out of military bases in neighboring Mozambique and Zambia. In 1976, the two organizations linked up in the political arena, calling themselves the ZANU-PF, and continued to fight their political battle against the Rhodesian Front.

Finally, by 1979, after more disputes, all parties were willing to come to the bargaining table. An agreement between white and black representatives took place at Lancaster House in London (known as The Lancaster House Accords), and gained the approval of the United Nations.[28] Specific compromises penned into the Lancaster House Accords allowed whites to be guaranteed twenty seats (for seven years only) in the newly formed Parliament, while blacks were allowed to elect eight representatives to the remaining seats. More importantly, twenty-five years after independence, Zimbabwe's black majority finally gained the right to vote. Robert Mugabe, head of the new ZANU-PF party, was elected Prime Minister in April 1980, and he appointed a cabinet that included ZANU and white Rhodesian Front members, as a gesture of reconciliation.[29] Yet it was clear that Ian Smith's party had lost nearly all of its political power.

The Lancaster House Accords also included a key measure for the commercial farmers: It protected property rights in the Constitution, and stipulated that any land acquired by the government for the purposes of land redistribution had to be purchased on a "willing seller-willing buyer" basis. At the last minute, a key provision was added: All compensation to the landowner would have to be made in foreign exchange. The Accords thus provided tremendous security to the landowners because any change in the Constitution regarding property rights required a unanimous vote of Parliament members. At the same time, it put the new government in an awkward position when trying to fulfill campaign promises of rectifying past inequities. Land redistribution was going to be extremely expensive, at least for the next ten years.

However, after ten years the Lancaster agreement would expire, and then the Zimbabwean Parliament could change property rights laws with a two-thirds vote, effectively cutting out the white voting bloc. Unbeknownst to the Zimbabwean people, their economic fortunes hinged more on property rights laws than they could have imagined.

The Path of the New Mugabe Government.

After elections in 1980, Robert Mugabe's ZANU-PF government faced a tremendous need to redress racial inequities after 15 years of civil unrest. Mugabe had openly socialist goals that were hostile to the laws of the free market, although he recognized that the quicker the goals were pursued, the more it would cost. There was a balancing act, to be sure, between steering the country towards a socialist model, but not greatly damaging the Zimbabwe's economic engine in the process. Immediate changes included the following:[30]

- Minimum wages were set, as were maximum increases.
- Taxes were increased to finance a new and improved health and education system.
- Laws were put in place that made it more difficult to fire workers.
- Communal farmers gained access to cheap credit and subsidized fertilizer, and roads and marketing depots (government buying locations for crops) were built in the communal areas.
- Strict price controls were applied to control inflation.

Few were satisfied with these changes. But they fell in line with the three long-term objectives of the government. First, ZANU-PF sought to consolidate state power and create conditions of peace and national unity. Second, it planned to reverse past discriminatory practices in land distribution, by putting more of the desirable, white-held land in the control of black Zimbabweans. Third, it aimed to lay down the political, economic and social bases for a transition to socialism.

The pursuit of these goals would ultimately damage the institution of free markets and private property rights for Mugabe's subsequent five presidential terms. Nationalizing industries meant the economy misses out on the multiplier effect that occurs through leveraging private property. Consolidating state power meant nationalizing industries would make it difficult for individuals to challenge the government when property rights and other freedoms were taken away.

On the first count, the government did very well, as ZANU-PF became the dominant and usually unchallenged political party. In general, the ZANU-PF represented the Shona, who made up 70 percent of Zimbabwe's 11 million people. The opposing party, PF-ZAPU represented the Nbebele, which constituted 17 percent of the total population. Whites, or the "European" population, numbered around 200,000.[31] By 1989 the two parties had formally merged under ZANU-PF.

With regard to the second policy, land reform, the Mugabe government initially looked to the British to pay the white farmers for their land, in light of British Rhodes' former colonial pursuits. After Britain showed great reluctance, Mugabe's approach during the first two years was to have the government purchase the white-owned land at market prices, in order to give this land to black farmers.[32] The pace was slow, however, and aggravated many of his supporters.

The economy's effort to nationalize property and assets, a goal of socialism, had been barred by the Lancaster House Constitution. However, the economy was very sophisticated relative to other countries in South Africa, with a high degree of industrialization, and good working trains and highways. Mugabe was focused on building upon, rather than tearing down these productive sectors of the economy.

Although Mugabe preached socialism, in fact he was continuing a strategy that had been led by Smith's government before him. For example, the government purchased shares of Zimbabwean companies to keep South African ownership (and influence) to a minimum.[33] Mugabe also sought to achieve more equity with regard to income distribution, and the largest obstacle standing in front of him was the vast wealth of land held by the whites. It seemed a natural path to push towards redistributing this land.

A Focus on Land Reform

Prior to the second election in 1985, Mugabe began denouncing the historical injustices of the commercial farming system and promised quicker land redistribution. It was an effective selling point in his political campaign. Yet as one observer noted, "Afterwards, political tempers seem to cool".[34] Mugabe won 76% of the votes, and the ZANU-PF winning 63 seats. Ian Smith's new Conservative Alliance of Zimbabwe won 15 of the 20 white seats, much to the displeasure of Mugabe.

To show that he was making good on his election pledges, Mugabe's government passed the Land Acquisition Act in late 1985. This Act made it mandatory for any commercial farmer considering a sale to first offer it to the government. A Derelict Lands Board was also established to take over under-utilized lands from commercial farmers. As a good politician, Mugabe could point to both of these actions as a sign that the government was serious about land reform. The reality was that not much happened.[35]

Even though the Mugabe government did not take much action, these actions signaled an ominous shift in the abstract notion of property rights. Rather than being seen as inviolate, property rights now meant a little less, since the government could usurp land when need be.

In other ways, Mugabe began to exercise and consolidate his political power. He dismissed two of the three whites in his cabinet, and as a result the white business community began edging away from Smith's coalition in favor of white independents. A new law granted Mugabe sweeping powers to deal with any urgent situation, involving defense, public order, safety, morality, health, or the economy.[36] Reports of widespread disregard for human rights began to appear more often.[37]

Then Mugabe's government abolished the twenty reserved white seats in Parliament in 1987, and replaced them with ZANU-PF nominees, half of whom were white. A constitutional amendment passed by the Parliament abolished the office of prime minister, and Mugabe was elected by the House of Assembly as the first executive president. The constitution also created a vice-presidential position, thus moving Zimbabwe closer to the United States form of government. Clearly, the power of commercial farming interests was waning.

Yet despite the government's consolidation of power, Mugabe did seem sensitive to public relations. For example, in 1989 five Ministers of Parliament purchased automobiles obtained at controlled government prices and resold them for huge profits on the black market. The public outcry at the national scandal provoked a response from Mugabe, and he fired all five of them, even though he shared close personal ties with two of the ministers.[38]

By 1989, elections were around the corner, and the political hot potato of land redistribution was heating up again. Through the 1980s, citizens criticized the Mugabe government again and again, for dragging its feet on land reform. Yet paying commercial farmers market prices was proving very expensive for the government, and it was running short of foreign exchange. Mugabe's rhetoric was now alarming commercial farmers, as he promised before the 1990 election to embark upon a "revolutionary land reform program, to redistribute land without inhibitions." Despite feverish lobbying by the farmers, Mugabe would not alter his views that the constitution's statements on property rights needed to be amended.[39] ZANU-PF politicians traveled the countryside prior to the elections, promising that 5 million hectares of commercial farmland would be expropriated by the government, with the goal of settling 162,000 black families on prime farmland owned by four thousand white farmers.

On April 18th, 1990, the Lancaster House agreement expired, setting the stage for the future of property rights, and the future economic course for Zimbabwe. The elections, also held in April, led to Mugabe's re-election to a third five-year term, with nearly 80% of the votes cast for him. Immediately afterwards, the commercial farmers mobilized with their lobby group, the Commercial Farmers' Union (CFU), to protest what looked like inevitable land redistribution. The Mugabe government was now considering different ways to put the land in the hands of more blacks, given that the government budget was tight. These possibilities included a land tax, placing restrictions on individuals from more than one farm, and not allowing foreigners to own farms. The Commercial Farmers' Union argued that this would interfere with property rights and "scare away the very foreign investors that the government was then trying to attract."[40]

Despite these arguments, Witness Mangwende, the Minister of Agriculture, gave commercial farmers little solace. "There was no going back," he said.[41] The major constraint on land redistribution had been the Lancaster House agreement. The government was now free to choose its own course.

In December 1990, a constitutional amendment was rushed through parliament. The amendment was significant in how much it weakened property rights for commercial farmers. Prior to 1990, farmers' compensation for land would be "prompt" and payment would be "adequate." Now the amendment said that the time to pay would be "reasonable" and the compensation would be "fair." The amendment was vague in how this would be spelled out; it allowed for future legislation to determine the rules for acquisition and compensation.[42] The most controversial aspect of the amendment was an attempt by the government to stamp out any questions from the courts about the fairness of the compensation. The clause read, "no such law shall be called into question by any court on the ground that the compensation provided by that law is not fair."[43] This clause was later removed, but again showed Mugabe's growing disregard for the institution of property rights.

Matters then grew worse for commercial white farmers. The Land Acquisition Act of 1992 passed which allowed the government to expropriate land without permission at a price set by the government. The dropping of the "willing seller-willing buyer clause" was vehemently opposed by the CFU. The CFU supported the idea of land reform, but believed the issue should be settled in an arbitration court using qualified persons, rather than political appointees. The bill attempted to make good on Mugabe's promise for land redistribution, but of course it did so at a far lower cost than previous purchases. By 1992, over 70 large-scale farms were designated for redistribution, with twenty-seven farms taken against the owners' will. The government pointed out that this was a small fraction of the 4,300 large-scale farms that had the richest and most valuable land.[44]

Mugabe now repeatedly called for Zimbabwe to become a one-party state, with a drive towards having a permanent lock on his leadership position, although the coalition government did not approve this. In 1996 elections were held again, and this time Mugabe won 93% of the vote, in elections where only 1 in 3 people bothered to vote.[45] Many people, including urban middle class blacks, were growing increasingly cynical and angry about the corruption apparent in the Mugabe regime, which repaid its supporters and high-ranking politicians (including former Minister of Agriculture Witness Mangwende) with prime pieces of farming real estate taken from the commercial farmers. Many of these farms were then left underutilized and suffered from neglect.[46] The workers employed by the farms, primarily black, then suffered as well, as they lost their jobs. Unemployment was skyrocketing, and promises of land redistribution were seen as nothing more than "callow promises by politicians intent on whipping up support for the next election."[47]

In late 1998 the government began "playing the card of the anti-Imperialist Freedom fighter." In an address by Mugabe to prospective voters in the Matobo District in September of that year, Mugabe spoke of "rich farm lands in former white colonial hands", and explained that farm occupations by government would be a way to "cure the economic and social ills bedeviling the nation."[48]

Britain had long acknowledged the urgent need for land reform, and spent 44 million pounds on the effort during the 1980s. However, the British government became increasingly frustrated with reports that Zimbabwean political officials and other influential people were using the land reform measures to their advantage, in some cases even pushing poor settlers off the land for their own uses.[49] As an example of this, the Mugabe government purchased 200 farms using British money in the mid 1990s and then distributed them to loyal army officers and party officials. One giant estate was parceled into 27 smaller farms and presented to a handful of party figures, including presidential spokesman George

Charamba. General Vitalis Zvinavashe received his own estate while thousands of poor Zimbabweans on waiting lists were ignored.[50] As Zeilig (2002) notes, "In the recent land grab it is again political patronage that has determined allocation. Loyal reporters, leading politicians and soldiers have been given land, but title deeds have remained with the government, ensuring continued loyalty to the regime."[51]

A British Embassy document stated, "We deplore the approach adopted to recent land reform which has disrupted commercial and communal farming alike, and which has been violent and unfair to farm owners and farm workers, and damaging to agricultural production and the national economy."[52] Britain's major concerns in 1999 were that Zimbabwe was not adhering to principles established at a donor conference in 1998, which included respect for the law and sound economic management. By 2000, Britain stopped the monetary support for land reform program, but continued to support land resettlement through the private sector. These small-scale measures never received governmental clearance, however.[53]

By February 2000, voters were fed up with the failing economy and what they saw as a corrupt government. They rejected Mugabe's call for a new constitution, which would have further entrenched Mugabe's executive powers. Prior to the April Presidential election, Mugabe's government used threats, intimidation and harassment in a "reign of terror" designed to kowtow the opposition party from winning. Closely watched by world political observers, the Movement for Democratic Change (MDC) nearly defeated Mugabe's Zanu-PF party, despite tough odds. MDC leader Morgan Tsvangirai, who received 42% of the vote, versus Mugabe's 56%, called the elections "massively rigged." Tsvangirai launched a court challenge, contending abduction of polling agents, fraud, and manipulation of voters' rolls.[54] The government countered by formally charging Tsvangirai with plotting a conspiracy against the government.

Ignoring the constitutional provisions after his re-election, on July 15, 2000 the Mugabe government launched the so-called "Fast Track" program, which was put in all eight provinces in the country. The following land was identified for resettlement:

- derelict farms
- under-utilized farms
- over-sized farms, that threatened ecological stability
- farms belonging to absentee landlords
- farms adjacent to communal areas
- farms under multiple ownership.

Local committees made up of traditional leaders, councilors, government administrators, representatives of war veterans and other special appointments carried out the selection. The committee was "meant to ensure that beneficiaries of the Land Resettlement Program were the landless and disadvantaged sector of the population."[55] Of course, the interpretation of words like "derelict", "under-utilized" and "over-sized" meant that any commercial farm could probably fit into one of the above categories. Sixteen days later the government announced that additional farms would be acquired, bringing the total to 3,041. There was now no need to justify land reform by earmarking so-called inefficient farms. All of them were now legally available.

Several court rulings tested the legality of the government's land reform program, and in December 2000, the Supreme Court declared the fast-track land reform unconstitutional. Mugabe simply replaced unfriendly judges, and in December 2001 the ruling was overturned. Another High Court judge ruled that Mugabe could not order evictions of white farmers, as banks held the titles to the land, and the government had not notified these banks. In response, the Mugabe government amended the Land Acquisition Act and vastly increased penalties for non-compliance. On September 18, 2002, Parliament approved the amendments and the government reissued eviction notices to white farmers, giving them seven days to leave.[56]

Since the year 2000 about 11 million hectares of commercial farm properties have been "gazetted" for acquisition by the government under the Land

Acquisition Act. This comprised 99 percent of the freehold land, and this has effectively nationalized nearly all the property in the agricultural sector. Yet few white farmers have surrendered the title deeds to their properties because of the "ridiculously low" levels of compensation being offered, and many of the farm acquisitions are tied up in litigation, according to an economist at the CFU.[57]

Mugabe did not forget those who had voted for him. In late October 2002, prior to local council elections, and in the face of tremendous food shortages, the ZANU-PF officials reportedly seized maize from the World Food Program's partner, and distributed it to pro ZANU-PF voters.[58] Calls for Mugabe's resignation now began to resonate from various quarters of Zimbabwe, but he stubbornly remained in power, despite a country crumbling around him.

By the end of 2003, 4,000 white families had left under great duress, some moving to neighboring African countries, and others to Australia or England. As they left, another precious yet intangible commodity was lost: The knowledge and skills needed to wrest a bounty of crops from an inherently difficult farming region. Complex irrigation systems and sophisticated pesticide control once created more food than Zimbabweans consumed, nearly all on the commercial-owned farms. With the farms now being carved up into hundreds of thousands of small-scale plots, the "scratch the surface" methods returned Zimbabwe to pitifully small yields. Agricultural output in 2002 plummeted to only 30 percent of what it was in the 2000, forcing Zimbabwe to rely on handouts from United Nations food programs.[59]

With a serious drop in food exports (a $600 million drop in tobacco alone[60]), far less money was available for imports, leaving the economy in a shambles. Inflation ran between 200-500% in 2002.[61] Shortages of the most basic commodities, such as maize meal, sugar, cooking oil, milk and salt were commonplace. Violence escalated as food grew scarcer.[62] Since 2000, the balance of trade deficit worsened by nearly six-fold, from $194 million to $1.1 billion, as investors trampled each other to get their money out of the country. By 2002, half of its 12 million population was facing starvation.[63]

Table 2.1. Key Legislative Acts and Events Affecting Land and Property Rights in Zimbabwe, 1889-2004

Legislation or event (date)	Summary
The Lippert Concession (1889)	Allowed would-be settlers to acquire land rights from the indigenous people. This resulted in the Rhodes' British South Africa Company buying concessions from Britain, which was then used as a basis for land expropriation. The indigenous people received no revenue for the land.
The Native Reserves Order in Council (1898)	Meant to prevent the extinction of large numbers of displaced indigenous people, by setting aside "native reserves", typically land in poor rainfall areas. These native reserves now make up the present day "communal areas."
1890-1920	During this period the BSAC seized 48,000,000 acres of land, along with another 13,000,000 by individual white European settlers. At this point 3% of the (white) population controlled 75% of the economically productive land.
The Land Apportionment Act (1930)	This act formally divided land between blacks and whites. The fertile high rainfall areas became large scale privately owned farms.
Lancaster House Conference (1979)	Meant to address imbalances between 3% of population (whites) owning 50% of the land. The conference sought to involve Britain in providing compensation for the white farmers, and giving them a ten-year grace period, before the Zimbabwean government could push forward with more aggressive land reform measures.
POST INDEPENDENCE	
The Communal Land Act (1981)	This act's intention was to shift the authority for property rights from tribal leaders to local authorities.
The Land Acquisition Act (1985)	This gave the government the first right to purchase large scale commercial farms for resettlement of indigenous people. Farms could only be voluntarily sold under the "willing buyer-willing seller" principle.
The Land Acquisition Act (1992)	A follow-up to the 1985 Act, meant to acquire more land for blacks. Farmland that was designated as derelict, under-utilized, "over-sized" compulsorily acquired by government.
Land reforms, 2000-2004	The Mugabe government declares in July 2000 that all white-owned farmland would be subject to seizure by the government, with no compensation from the government, and loss of property titles.

Sources: Land Issue Fact Sheet, Zimbabwean government, and the Commercial Farmer's Union.

Intimidation of the Media and Increasing Isolation

After the Presidential election in 2002, Mugabe escalated the intimidation of the media.[64] Three journalists were arrested under a new media law in May 2002, and a suspicious bombing of an independent radio station occurred in August 2002.[65] The last remaining Western-based correspondent, writing for *The Economist*, was forced to leave the country in early 2003. Western journalists now had to pretend they were tourists to get into the country.[66] In October of 2003 government shut down Zimbabwe's *The Daily Mail* newspaper. The government claimed that because the staffers had not registered their party affiliation, they were in violation of existing law. The staffers were thrown in jail. This was the last media source in Zimbabwe still openly critical of the Mugabe government. Ironically, the last time a newspaper had been barred from operating was under the era of Ian Smith.[67] By January 2004 however, a court ordered the police to leave the offices of the *Daily Mail*, and as of this writing it is back in operation.[68]

Mugabe's increasingly anti-democratic, anti-market actions have earned him increasing ire and condemnation from other parts of the world. In March 2002, Zimbabwe was suspended from the Commonwealth after Britain and others complained amid widespread vote rigging, violence and political repression. The Commonwealth, a convening body representing some 1.7 billion people, has only suspended one member before- South Africa- because of the issues concerning apartheid policy.[69]

The significance of the decision for Zimbabwe is that it leaves behind a large voluntary organization that devotes itself to helping member countries in many social, economic, and technical areas, and promotes exchanges between highly skilled professionals. With Zimbabwe's exit, the number of member countries drops from to 53, and the challenge of finding a solution for its ills grows even greater.[70] In July 2002, the European Union ministers extended sanctions on the top seventy-two ZANU-PF government leaders, including Mugabe, freezing their access to European assets, and forbidding their travel within the EU.[71]

Given all the political problems that Zimbabwe faces, how easily might a healthy economy be reconstructed? As Milton Friedman has persuasively argued, markets thrive best in democratic environments.[72] The Zimbabwe government's repressive actions put it a long way from democracy. Yet there is a world of difference between Zimbabwe and say, North Korea. Zimbabwe was founded on democratic principles, from which it has only recently sharply diverged. North Korea has long been a brutal communist regime, with no built-in democratic mechanisms for due process. Thus it can be argued that Zimbabwe has far greater potential for getting back on track than does North Korea. To make this point, let us now explore Zimbabwe's government structure in more detail.

The Structure of the Government

National government

Although Zimbabwe declared itself a proponent of socialism in 1980, its federal government evolved by 1987 towards a system resembling the U.S. government structure. The Zimbabwe people are familiar with due process, a free press, free elections and a working judicial system, having had experience with it under the earlier years of the Mugabe government.

As in the U.S., Zimbabwe's president is the Head of State and also Commander-in-Chief of the Armed Forces. However, it was members of Zimbabwe's Parliament, not an electoral college, who elected the president for a term of five years. The national legislature, or Parliament, is composed of two bodies, the House of Assembly and the Senate. Zimbabwe's voters elect 120 of the 150 House members, with the other thirty representing appointments, chiefs of tribes and provincial governors. The Senate comprises forty members, with thirty-five elected by an electoral college, and the remaining five appointed by the President. As in the United States, a legislative bill first has to pass in the House and then in the Senate. Having passed there, it is presented to the President for his approval or veto. The federal government then obtains funding for its projects primarily from the income tax and sales tax.[73]

The President also has the power to appoint a group of twenty-two Ministers who form the Cabinet. Among them are the Minister of Health, the Minister of Higher Education, the Minister of Foreign Affairs, the Minister of Industry and Commerce, and the Minister of Defense. These Ministers advise the President on government matters and prepare legislation for consideration by Parliament.

The Constitution was approved by Great Britain's Parliament in 1979 and provided the legal foundation for the Zimbabwean government. Within its charter is contained the Declaration of Rights, similar to the United States Bill of Rights, guaranteeing among other things, freedom of expression, freedom of association and assembly, freedom from slavery, protection from discrimination on grounds of race, tribe, political opinion, color or creed. Constitutional amendments required at least a two-thirds vote in both the Senate and the House, with the key exception of the Lancaster House agreement on property rights. There, the vote needed to be unanimous.

In addition to protecting Zimbabweans politically, these freedoms provided an excellent backbone for well-functioning markets. When people can express and associate freely, and are protected from discrimination, this encourages people to form any business they please, without regard to political fallout. For example, media outlets do not need to worry about what information they sell, and employees from different tribes are assured they are being hired on account of their productivity and not their tribal background. Property can be bought and sold more freely as well, as the only aspect of the sale becomes the economic transaction, not the political ramifications of selling the property to, say someone outside the tribe, or to a well-known anti-government supporter. All of these political freedoms increase economic potential because they let resources flow to their highest valued economic use. Unfortunately, as these political freedoms and protections break down, so too the economy goes with it.

Local Government

While the federal government's legalistic structure enhanced the security of buying and selling of property, the local government depended upon the revenue from property taxes to run its daily operations. Local government provides representation for residents and is organized into commercial lands, urban areas, and communal lands.

Property rights laws were best defined in the urban areas. These areas raised most of their operating revenues by charging property taxes on all land in the council's area and by taxing motor vehicles. In urban areas, people elect urban councils, which generally provided a more sophisticated blend of public services than in the countryside. Besides maintaining roads, they are in charge of supplying electricity, sewer systems, ambulance and fire-fighting services, and collecting garbage.[74]

As in the United States, the commercial lands and urban areas had property of far higher value than the communal lands. This meant a higher revenue stream for the local councils, and disproportionately better level of services. These inequities heated up the calls for the land reform movement, and the ultimate disregard of many of the property rights laws.

When the Mugabe government began authorizing land seizures, the effect was to slowly disintegrate the trust and wealth created by property rights laws on both the national and local levels. The most devastating blow occurred in the agricultural sector, the backbone of the economy, with ripple effects spreading far and wide. Agriculture was the first tipped domino, and it is this sector to which we now turn.

Chapter 3. Conflicts Over Land: The History and Structure of the Agricultural Sector

Overview

Any visitor to Zimbabwe in the year 2000 would have been struck by the tremendous difference between the white-owned commercial farms on rich arable lands controlled by 4,500 farmers, and the dry, overworked and dusty communal farms owned by 840,000 black farmers. The white-owned farms had all the tools for world-class intensive farming techniques, including expensive irrigation systems, tractors and tilling equipment. The farmers also had sophisticated knowledge about how to squeeze the most crops out of the ground. Over half of the total land was located in high rainfall regions, which was far more suitable for crop production. But more importantly, the land was titled.

Neil Wright, head economist for the Commercial Farmers Union, stated in 2003:

> The commercial sub-sector was founded on, and developed as a consequence of farmers being able to mortgage their fixed properties and raise finance by providing financiers with mortgage bonds. This system of providing security for loans advanced to farmers was fundamental to being able to carry out farming operations within the commercial sub-sector, and to a large extent governed investment and output. It was the cornerstone to stimulating the entrepreneurial spirit that developed the sub-sector.[1]

Communal farmers had no such access to financial capital, and used primitive farming equipment, such as a crude plow, with no irrigation systems. The land was typically poorer, in large part because the farmers were forced onto those lands after the arrival of the Europeans. More than three-quarters of these farms were located in low rainfall regions. The overcrowding and lack of technology had made poor lands even more unyielding.[2]

In spite of the vast differences in the way the two groups farm, agriculture is the driving engine of the Zimbabwean economy. It only comprises 15 percent of GDP, yet it intimately linked with 60 percent of manufacturing output, since there are food processing, milling, beverage and textile industries (although manufacturing has been in a systemic decline.) Crops such as tobacco, maize and cotton account for 80 percent of agricultural production, with the other 20 percent coming from livestock.[3] Thus, the dramatic drop in agricultural yields since 2000 sent shock waves throughout the economy. Before examining the effects of those shock waves, let us first explore some background on this vital sector.

A Brief History Since 1965

In 1965, Zimbabwe (then Rhodesia) imported virtually all of its wheat. Facing international sanctions after the Unilateral Declaration of Independence (UDI) in 1967, Ian Smith's government decided to drastically change its agricultural public policy.

First, the agricultural sector was already relatively productive at the time of UDI, but tobacco accounted for 80% of agricultural output. Diversifying the agricultural sector through public policy measures was essential for self-sufficiency, the government believed. With the government providing price guarantees, subsidies and irrigation support, as well as low taxes, the commercial sector of agriculture expanded production of maize, wheat, beans, coffee, cotton and other crops. Tobacco production, meanwhile, fell dramatically to 24% of total agricultural production by 1969, although it crept back up to 32% by 1988.

Those policies proved successful by some measures. By 1979 Zimbabwe (then Rhodesia) was producing 39% above its domestic needs for wheat, as well as harvesting plentiful yields in maize, cotton, sugar and tobacco. This was in contrast to the majority of African countries, which had to import large quantities of food.[4]

As described in Chapter 2, after the fall of Smith's government in 1980 the Mugabe-led government proceeded cautiously in land reform and public policy measures regarding land resettlement. The reason was straightforward. In 1980, the commercial, white-dominated sector accounted for 75% of gross agricultural output, nearly 100% of agricultural export earnings, and 33% of the economy's formal wage employment. Clearly, the new government did not want to thwart all the gains during the past 15 years. Yet politically, Mugabe had a problem, given the gross inequities in land ownership and productivity between blacks and whites. The real problem for the state (to the present day) was how to transfer more land into the hands of blacks, especially the communal farmers, without sacrificing the efficiency and productivity of the commercial farms.[5] Ten percent of the commercial farms created fifty percent of all the agricultural production. The most important ingredient in these high performing farms was their extensive use of capital equipment and knowledge of high-yield farming methods. Both of these are difficult to transfer without extensive training and education.

In addition, prospects for land redistribution were constrained by legal issues. As discussed earlier, the clause in the Lancaster House Agreement forbade the expropriation of land for redistributive purposes, so all land purchased from individuals was voluntarily sold by the owner, and paid for in foreign currency. Zimbabwe originally wanted Britain to compensate the white farmers for the loss of their land, but the money never came. The resulting impact of land redistribution measures through the 1980s was "marginal," benefiting less than 7% of the communal farmers.[6] By 1986, the government had purchased 2.6 million hectares of land from commercial farmers. Only 130,000 hectares had been used to resettle families.[7] Originally the government planned to resettle 162,000 families in three years. But many commercial farmers were not willing to sell their land at government offered prices, so the plan fell short.[8] As of 1988, only 40,000 of the 700-800,000 families living in communal areas had been resettled.[9] As discussed earlier, a bill passed in late December 1990 allowed the government to expropriate land from the white farmers without paying the full market value, to the detriment of agricultural output, foreign investment, and confidence in government institutions.

Differences in Land Ownership Prior to the Land Seizures of 2000-2003.

As we have seen, Zimbabwe's agricultural sector was divided into two sub-sectors, commercial and communal. Prior to 2000, the commercial sub-sector had about 5,400 large-scale farms, covering 15.6 million hectares of land area. As of 1985, only 4,800 of those farms were actively farmed. These farms were highly capital-intensive as well as having the richest soil and best crop yields. Whites owned over 90% of them. There were also large discrepancies in land holding among individuals in large- scale farming. For example, 60% of all land in this sector was owned by only 10% of the farmers.[10] The commercial sub-sector also included small-scale commercial farms, covering 1.5 million hectares and occupied by about 9,000 black families. Originally blacks leased these lands but now many are owned.[11] Under pressure from the government, the Commercial Farmers' Union (CFU), representing white farming interests, merged in 1981 with the Zimbabwe National Farmers' Union (ZNFU), which represented small-scale black commercial farmers.[12] Both of these sectors had property titles attached to their land. This meant shared values concerning the value of land equity, and of the power of borrowing against it for purchase of seeds, equipment and the like.

But the CFU would not hear of merging with the Zimbabwe National Farmers' Association of Zimbabwe (NFAZ), which represented communal farmers. Not only would 200,000 communal farmers instantly outvote the CFU's 4,500 farmers, but their perception of property rights was sharply different as well. This difference in outlook continues to this day and is worth investigating in more detail.

Property rights in the communal lands

For a Westerner, there is a clear impression of openness across much of the African landscape. This is partially due to its history of agriculture and the way property rights have been defined. As we have seen, following colonialism, black Zimbabweans were forced to move to the poorer agricultural lands, while the white Europeans snared the lands with richer soils and higher rates of rainfall.

However, what is not usually mentioned is that communal farming methods would have eventually depleted those richer soils anyway. Communal farming methods are a recipe for disaster, and the results have already manifested themselves in the three years since commercial lands has been converted to communal ones.

Traditionally, communal lands have been cleared by fire, and crops planted by hand, by throwing seeds into the dirt. Neighboring forests are chopped down to make room for more farmland, and provide fuel for heat and cooking. This short-term approach robs the soil of important nutrients, and increases erosion. When the farmland's soil is exhausted, the communal farmers move on to the next region. Furthermore, in communal lands there are no leases or title to land, so there is little incentive for individuals to conserve or greatly invest in either their land or their home. This is a textbook example of "tragedy of the commons", which describes the overuse of any resource that no one owns.[13]

Tragedy of the commons becomes a larger problem when people encroach upon the land and live closer together, which is typical of any growing economy. As this happens, property rights become more important as a way to prevent the overuse of resources. For example, poachers nearly caused the white rhino to go extinct on the plains of Mozambique, and cowboys nearly killed all the buffalo on the Great Plains of the United States. No one owned them, so they were not conserved or cared for. In contrast, the elephant population now thrives in Zimbabwe, one of the few countries in Africa where this is true. This is because the government allows Zimbabweans the right to own them, just as they own livestock. Making elephants valuable to Africans by allowing them to trade in their products is a way to ensure the species' sustainable existence. Now villagers take care of their elephants rather than seeing them as a nuisance that tramples their crops, which previously gave them an incentive to shoot them.[14]

But Zimbabwe does not follow this important lesson with its communal land. Indeed, wealthy urbanites have taken advantage of this "free good", by purchasing large numbers of livestock, and placing them on open communal land for free grazing, and coming by for a visit on weekends. The people living nearby have no way to regulate this oversupply of animals, and invariably the land gets overgrazed and exhausted. Then it is time to move on, to turn to the next forest to chop down, the next field to burn.[15]

Thus, there is little attempt to use the land as a renewable resource. The Western idea of land ownership is a foreign concept. One white farmer told a story of his grandfather going to see a local chief about buying some land many years ago. "Buy land?" said the chief. "You must be crazy — you don't buy the wind or the water or the trees!"[16] This story still resonates in present-day Zimbabwe.

Today in the communal lands a tension now simmers between recognizing modern day property rights and maintaining traditional customs. Embracing modern day property rights means embracing potential for change. Traditional village life is far less subject to change when it is difficult to buy and sell property. Land is not readily available to outsiders. It is striking to consider that it is the traditional property rights system that ties people to the village, to their land, and to a way of life that has not changed in hundreds of years.

How has this tension been created? For centuries in Zimbabwe, the traditional tribal leaders (sabbukkus) allocated the use of land to people in the village, on the basis of the leader's judgement, and the villager's influence. This gave tribal leaders tremendous power to both gain and give privileges to the villagers. It also put villagers in a subservient position, anxious about offending the sabbukku lest he remove their rights to their land.

In 1982, the Mugabe government passed the Communal Lands Act, which attempted to replace this informal process with a more formal process of having villagers elect officials to serve on a Village Development Committee (VIDCO). The idea of the VIDCOs was to create more egalitarian life in the village, by allocating villagers individual and uniform plots of land. However, villagers were rankled by the "top-down" approach. It failed to recognize their customs and traditions. In practice, the official process and the traditional process remained in conflict with each other, resulting in power struggles between government officials and the sabbukkus.

In addition, Nyambara (2001), in a comprehensive study of communal property laws, found that in Zimbabwe's Gokwe district, immigrants, squatters and established villagers frequently squabbled over unevenly enforced land rights. Sabbukkus often used their prestige as village headsmen to allocate more land to themselves. The result has been growing "land anarchy" and struggles for power. In addition, the villagers could obtain land through the secret "informal" land market, bypassing official land allocation requirements. In many cases and places, Baker (1989) found that chiefs and other local leaders were able to turn the right of land allocation into the rights of personal allocation, and have been able to amass both cash and large land holdings.[17]

According to Moyo (1995), less and less land is expressly communal, that is, owned by all the community. Today, 'communal' lands are often those lands in rural areas that are not formally titled, but are allocated under the good graces of the sabbukku. Cash transactions by outsiders are becoming more common, but this is not done on an open basis. Rather, it resembles bribes to the village heads. Nyambara (2001) reports that local villagers wrote numerous letters to the Gokwe rural district council complaining about the increase in cash transactions for village land, paid to the sabbukku by recent immigrants. These letters convey the sense that cash transactions are "unfair". In another telling case, a village head was particularly notorious for selling land to immigrants. Letters went back and forth between him and the local VIDCO. When summoned to the office, the village head "declared that the land belonged to him to do as he pleased with."[18]

Other Complexities in Communal Property Rights Laws

As we have seen, complicated property rights laws hinder development, and also lower the value of property. In Zimbabwe's villages, the complications come from a variety of factors. For example, a household could have exclusive rights for cultivation of crops on agricultural land, but at the same time, indigenous trees bearing fruit could be common property. At the same time, in some villages households may collect this fruit for gifts, but may not resell it. Any natural water supply is also communal property. Some areas are marked for communal grazing by the village animals, which can often lead to overgrazing.[19]

Yet these local property laws also recognize the value-added concept. For an allocated property, households may grow crops or trees, and make their own decisions concerning planting, protection and harvesting. They have the rights to exclude others from the work they have created. The common thread that runs through this maze of laws is that if you have worked for it, you may keep it. If nature has provided it, such as indigenous trees, fallen firewood, free-flowing streams, meadows, and so on, then that is the village's communal property, from which all may benefit.

That sounds appealing and equitable, but like most shared resources, it tends to be overused. In a village with little economic growth, this is less of an issue, but inevitably population growth in any country will put a strain on resources. The search for firewood becomes longer each year, the meadows become overgrazed, and so on.

There is now strong evidence of widespread "resource degradation" in Zimbabwe, because of the inability of these local laws to work effectively.[20] These local laws, while servicing the population for centuries, work best when there is a sense that there are plenty of resources for all. Once resources become "tight", communal property rights increase the likelihood that those resources will be overused, and even abused.

In addition to straining resources, multiple property rights systems create extremely high transactions costs for banks wishing to issue loans to individuals. This system is not dissimilar to the United States in the 1800s, where each bank issued its own currency, making it hard for people to transport their banknotes to another town with a different bank. Today, our universally accepted currency solves that problem. One of the ironies of industrialized societies in the West is how simple their property rights laws are in comparison to lesser-developed countries. That simplicity partially explains the differences in economic development.

A detailed case study: The Jina village

Each village in Zimbabwe has its own tailored property rights structure that reflects the joint desires of the people living there, the influence of the sabbuku, and the VIDCO. For example, take the Jina village, which is in the Manicaland province, in eastern Zimbabwe. Like many other villages in Zimbabwe, Jina has seen some formal changes in the distribution of property rights through the institution of its own VIDCO. In practice, little has changed. Kundhlande and Luckert described the complicated intersection of property rights of this village, which gives a good sense of the challenges facing Zimbabwe ahead in this area.[21]

Households in the Jina village have access to four different types of property rights: 1) Homestead land which is used to build their houses, 2) Agricultural land, used for growing crops, 3) garden plots, which can be located along river banks or in the homestead area, and 4) indigenous woodlands. Every household grows crops and has agricultural land. They also have common access to the indigenous woodlands, where they may collect firewood, or other forest products. (Collection of forest products does require paying a fee to the village authorities.) Crop stubble left in fields is left for roaming animals unless the field is fenced. In this case, villagers from open fields prohibit the villager with the fence from allowing his animals to graze on their lands.

Hunting small game and birds is allowed, but killing big game is prohibited. In another case of joint cooperation, villages from adjoining areas may have overlapping common areas, which offer different forest products. In these cases there is mutual agreement to share these common areas.

The sabbuku's role is still important in this village, despite the official transfer of authority from traditional leaders to VIDCOs. His influence extends to all four of the household rights, and VIDCOs and sabbukus have also found ways to cooperate and produce a single line of authority for property rights.

Limits on Property Rights, and Enforcement

One of the most important limits on these property rights in the Jina and other village is that they may not be sold to other households. As was explained in Chapter 2, these regulations depress the value of land in the village, adding to the tragedy of the commons' problems.

Agricultural land may be leased, but in this village, land disputes have led the sabbuku to discourage the practice. The only way for land rights to be transferred is to be given away, typically to family members. Giving land rights to outsiders requires the approval of the family, and the approval of the village authorities. The sabbuku is typically consulted as well. When the land is parceled out to family members, it becomes difficult for each successive generation to take advantage of scale farming techniques.

In a survey done in the Jina village, Kundhlande and Luckert found agreement that the growing population was putting increasing pressure on land resources, making it difficult to maintain communal areas. The respondents agreed that private property rights would become more common as time went on. In an area such as the Jina village (and of course elsewhere in Zimbabwe) where resources are getting ever scarce, there would be many ways for a communal area to be overused and even abused. One could steal vegetables from a garden plot along the river, have one's livestock graze on a neighbors' growing crop, or kill big game in the forest.

Thus, in widespread rural areas, there has to be either tremendous trust among villagers or another enforcement mechanism. The problem with using mutual trust is that while it is effective, it is exceedingly fragile. One incident of stolen vegetables could have the whole village guessing who was the culprit. It is here where the religious taboos and customs fulfill a vital regulatory role: Villagers believe that a person who breaks the rules will invite the wrath of the ancestors on that person, his family, or the entire village. The possibility that the entire village's fortunes could be ruined puts tremendous pressure on an individual to act in a responsible fashion. Guilt serves as an effective monitoring device.

In the case where an individual is either guiltless or doesn't believe the village lore about ancestor's wrath, he or she is also subject to being reported by other residents of the village. Depending on the severity of the offence, punishments range from the delivery of one chicken to the sabbuku, to brewing beer for the entire village. Typically a little extra libation is reserved to pour on the land to appease the ancestors. In any case, it is quite rare for authorities above the local level to become involved.

Given that this system of property rights creates a restraint on economic activity, and prevents villagers from realizing the full benefit of their investment in land resources, why haven't villagers rebelled against the system, as villagers did in the French revolution who fought for their property rights? The answer is that the present system, in place for centuries, must confer more perceived benefits than costs. By disallowing villagers from selling their land, this system prevents outsiders from intruding, and possibly disturbing village life. (In the U.S. people do the same thing when they buy into a housing development with multiple convenants, restricting everything from house colors to the size of a newly planted tree.) As in many villages around the world, people living there are more resistant to change than city dwellers. While some outsiders may see this as a binding restriction, most villagers probably view the rules as a necessary restraint to protect a way of life that is important to them. The ones who don't are most likely to move to urban areas, with less intrusive private property rights systems. However, it also raises the possibility that villagers may not fully comprehend the benefits of transferable property, but simply accept the system because this is always how it has been done.

Differences in land ownership: Zimbabwe viewed from outer space

Today, more than 800,000 farmers and their families live on crowded communal farms, having no property titles. Blacks were crowded onto the comparatively poorer soil by the white Europeans, as discussed in Chapter 2, but since Rhodes' conquest the soil has progressively gotten much worse; sixty percent is classified as poor or very poor soil. The combination of the "tragedy of the commons" and overcrowding has led to 75% of the communal land lying fallow at any given time. [22] A recent survey concluded nearly one-quarter of the lands are severely eroded.[23]

NASA satellite photos in the center of this book show striking evidence of this degradation, even when Africa is viewed as a whole. In the midst of green vegetation, Zimbabwe's land degradation is clearly visible as a small light patch on the lower right. In the succeeding photos of Zimbabwe, it is easy to spot the communal lands versus the commercial lands. The communal lands snake north to south through Zimbabwe; they are composed of the smaller clusters of squares, which are scuffed in appearance and whitish tan, indicating severe lack of vegetation. There is no difference in their coloration regardless of whether they are in the northern high rainfall areas, or the drought-prone southern areas.

In contrast, the larger squares consist of commercial lands or national parks, and are various tones of a healthy green. These lands, with far fewer individuals living on them, and often irrigated, indicate that commercial farming can flourish even under dry conditions.

Research by geographer Stephen Prince indicates that the communal lands are in low-productivity areas, but they still under-produce their potential, due to "inappropriate" land practices and severe overcrowding. There is even evidence that the communal farming practices have changed weather patterns, increasing the level of drought conditions because of the lack of vegetation in these areas. Small-scale commercial farming, done primarily by blacks, also has been successful in preventing the erosion caused by communal farming, as the succeeding satellite photos reveal. Those areas are little different from the large-scale zones, having a light shade of green.[24] However, land reform has caused many of these green commercial zones to turn the color of the communal farm zones, a result of the loss of property rights. (Table 3.1 shows the tremendous differences in ownership of land, which gave Mugabe political grist in arguing for land reform.)

Table 3.1. Differences in Farming Area by Type of Farmer Prior to 2000.[25]

Large-scale commercial	**Small-scale commercial**	**Communal**	**Resettlement**
4,800 farms	8,500 farms	800,000 plots	300,000 plots
12.8 million hectares	1.4 million hectares	16.4 million hectares	2.6 million hectares
Largely white-owned	Black-owned	Black-owned	Black-owned
Average size per farm: 2,667 hectares, but top 10% of farms averaged 16,042 hectares.	Average size per farm: 165 hectares.	Average size per farm: 21 hectares.	Average size per farm: 8 hectares.

Production differences

There are also differences in production. The communal farms, using poorer soils, grow a variety of crops, ranging from maize, cotton, groundnuts, sorghum and sunflower seeds. Many communal farms also rely on income from family members working elsewhere. Commercial farms, meanwhile, depend more on cash crops for export, such as tobacco, cotton, sugar, and horticulture, but also produce substantial quantities of maize and wheat.[26] Looking at the Table 3.3 below shows the differences in production for Zimbabwe's most important crops, as well as the changes in their production levels over the years. The largest differences in terms of types of crops planted were in sugarcane production and groundnuts. The commercial farmers did all the profitable sugarcane, wheat and tobacco crop production, whereas the communal farmers did nearly all of the labor-intensive groundnut production, as seen in Table 3.3. Commercial farms are typically irrigated. Moreover, the most lucrative cash crop, tobacco, is far more resistant to drought than other crops. Communal farmers' fortunes are more closely aligned with the weather and the amount of rainfall. Water, or the lack of it, ties most Zimbabweans to their present and future more than any other scarce resource.

Table 3.2. Commercial and Communal Agricultural Production, in 1000s of tons

Crop	1996/97	1997/98	1998/99	1999/2000	2000/01	2001/02
Tobacco,						
commercial	162	210	186	178	186	154
communal	2	3	3	5	4	19
Maize,						
commercial	825	573	662	675	482	186
communal	1,397	577	944	939	994	315
Cotton,						
commercial	64	61	48	46	52	10
communal	191	157	149	195	234	180
Sugarcane,						
commercial	2,075	1,487	1,186	2,261	537	n/a
communal	0	0	0	0	0	0
Wheat,						
commercial	245	232	286	250	n/a	115
communal	7	2	1	1	n/a	98
Groundnuts,						
commercial	13	8	9	9	16	2
communal.	143	51	71	112	156	57

Source: Commercial Farmers Union.

The Importance of Water

Water is a serious enough issue in Africa to have a conference named for it.[27] Africa has the smallest percentage of people who have access to water in the entire world. The high variability of rainfall and relatively small amount of runoff create frequent droughts and floods. Constant migration by African tribes over the centuries was a coping mechanism for these highly variable conditions, and probably was one of the reasons why property rights were not well defined.

To exacerbate matters, the carving up of Africa by the English, French, Belgians and Germans during the last two centuries resulted in country borders that focused on access to mineral rights rather than water rights. The result was that every country in Africa now shares at least one river basin. There are over 60 shared river basins in Africa, more shared basins than any other continent.

Zimbabwe's fortunes are tied to rainfall, and the extreme variability means a large potential for loss. To solve this problem, better water resource management (such as building large dams, irrigation and zoning for watershed areas) is needed. The overriding issue, however, is not dams or irrigation, but how the property rights and access to water are controlled, on both domestic and international fronts. The droughts and variability in rainfall are issues that can be addressed with irrigation, technology and insurance markets. But first, water needs to be treated as a scarce resource with a price attached to it.

In Zimbabwe and the rest of Africa, stewardship of shared water basins can be accomplished by first agreeing on the economic benefits of the shared water supply. Then it is the responsibility of each government to insure that the water is managed correctly. The United States, Japan and The European Union have made similar international agreements with regard to fishing rights in the world's oceans, to prevent overexploitation of the underwater resources. The World Bank is presently working with African countries towards those water resource goals, but has many obstacles ahead.

Zimbabwe and other African countries will benefit the most if the World Bank focuses first on helping these countries create well-defined property rights structures for all of their natural resources. Important questions such as "Who should own the water?" and "How does one decide on a price for water?" need ferreting out. Although certainly less glamorous than building large-scale hydroelectric dams, the hard work of countries coming together on such vital matters is essential.

So why do the United States and other donor countries support World Bank projects that persist in investing huge sums of money on large -scale projects such as dams, rather than beginning with the basics? Some have argued that the reason is leverage. The World Bank, by offering large scale "goodies," can also threaten to take them away if the government "misbehaves." The United States, as a principal donor to The World Bank, can use the millions of dollars spent in foreign aid as a way to peddle "soft influence" around the world to advance its own interests.[28]

Today, however, Zimbabwe's biggest threat is not from the outside, but from itself. The collapse of the agricultural sector happened with such speed that it is worth viewing it in slow motion, as it were, to better assess the mechanics of the collapse. It is to this story to which we now turn.

Chapter 4. Government Agricultural Policies: What Happened?

Overview

From Zimbabwe's own government policies to those of The World Bank, well-intentioned policy-makers left Zimbabwe worse off than before by the year 2000. In some cases it was the result of protectionist and socialist policies that distorted the efficiency of the market mechanisms, leading to chronic shortages and surpluses. In other cases, "cold-turkey" reform policies aggravated underlying structural deficiencies. These ill-timed policies left Zimbabwe particularly vulnerable to economic collapse when the land seizures began taking place. In addition, Mugabe's government used the drought during 2000-2003 as a convenient scapegoat for falling agricultural yields, which was accepted rather uncritically by some at the World Bank as an important mitigating factor. The role of this chapter is to describe how those policies aggravated the circumstances of a severe drought, turning what could have been a serious but manageable problem into a catastrophe.

The Role of Government Pricing Policy

Much has been written about the success of Zimbabwe's agricultural program during the 1980s, in light of the failed agricultural programs in many other African Countries. With an agricultural yield of some crops that was the best in the world, and one of the few African countries that was relatively self-sufficient in food, it appeared Zimbabwe's agricultural planning boards had accomplished more than most others. But it is also worth exploring some of the costs of government intervention during this time. After all, the pertinent question should not be how well Zimbabwe did relative to the rest of Africa, but rather, how well it did relative to its potential.

Every major crop in Zimbabwe, as well as dairy and beef products, was subject to price controls. Price controls have been part of Zimbabwe's farming economy since the 1930s.[1] Marketing boards decide "fair prices" at the level of food processing as well as the retail markets, by analyzing cost data. This is done on an annual basis. Both commercial and communal farmers become heavily involved in the price negotiations. Some crops, such as maize, have a long history of being regulated by the government; others have been controlled only recently, corresponding with their introduction into the agricultural sector.

There are four government boards, sometimes called "parastatals": The Grain Marketing Board (GMB), the Cold Storage Commission (CSC), the Cotton Marketing Board (CMB) and the Dairy Marketing Board (DMB). Farmers criticized these organizations for not paying the world price for their products, but when those world prices declined, not surprisingly, they "rallied around the system."[2] Through the mid 1970s, the boards operated on a not-for-profit status, but in the late 1970s the boards began to run large deficits. This was because the boards purchased the crops at a higher price than they sold them to the public. With the advent of the Mugabe government, the volatility of world crop prices kept the marketing boards from running a no profit-no loss budget. It became increasingly difficult to figure out where prices were heading next, and the GMB ran continual deficits within the first few years of the Mugabe administration.

As with most countries having controlled prices, long-term shortages and surpluses are not uncommon in Zimbabwe. In the early to mid 80s, the price structure favored the production of maize over more drought-resistance crops such as sorghum and millet.[3] This exacerbated the food shortages during dry spells, necessitating imports of 200,000 tons of maize.[4] When the rains finally did arrive in 1984-85 and the succeeding crop year, favorable prices for farmers led to an enormous stockpile, which could not be handled by either storage facilities or foreign markets.

Later attempts by the government to intervene in the agricultural market further increased the country's vulnerability to drought and reduced productivity. In the name of "fair" prices, a two-tier price for maize was introduced in late 1986 by the government. Under the new system, smaller, less productive farmers earned more money per ton than the larger producers. The following crop year, maize sales fell by 13% in a year where overall crop sales had risen by nearly 9%. In 1987/88 during a minor drought, maize sales plummeted 75%, their lowest level in years.[5] Zimbabwe, once able to feed itself, was now only producing 90 percent of the food per capita in the three years 1987-89, as compared to the three year period 1979-1981.[6] The GMB's slowness in adjusting to prices meant that in the mid 1980s, commercial farmers turned away from maize production, citing low guaranteed prices, rising costs of production and more profitable alternatives, despite excess demand by consumers.

As well as controlling marketing and producer prices, some of the other government regulatory responsibilities included management of irrigation, extension of loans towards commercial (and more recently) communal farmers. All of the main crops and animal products were sold through five marketing boards, which manage tobacco, cotton, grain and coffee, dairy, and pork products. These boards typically lost money; for example, by 1989 the Cotton Marketing Board had accumulated a deficit of 35 million Zimbabwean dollars.[7]

Using the example of maize will show how these deficits easily occurred. The GMB bought all the maize farmers produce at a guaranteed Z$195 (as of 1989) per ton. It sold the maize on the domestic market at $245 per ton. Yet after adding in government distribution costs, the board loses Z$35 per ton, after selling the maize. In addition, if there is a surplus that must be sold on the world market, typically the world price for maize is less than half the supported price. An accumulated Z$44 million deficit for this program by 1989 was the result of such a policy. Agricultural subsidies arise mainly because the board's selling prices are not always high enough to cover producer costs and board costs.

The Mugabe government appeared aware of the problems caused by subsidies, and in a report lamented that this program led to lower levels of capital investment than otherwise.[8] In addition, the report acknowledges high-income earners may receive a greater proportion of the subsidy benefit because they purchase greater quantities of the goods. The poorest of the poor living in rural areas may have little access to these subsidized products. Thus, the subsidies "tend to accrue more to consumer groups who may not be primary targets of policy." The total government expenditure on supporting the agricultural sector in 1988/89 was 6.3% of the total budget, or 318 million Zimbabwean dollars.[9] From the accumulated debt from 1981 to 1989 was a "staggering" Z$814 billion.[10]

As with any government price control system, those who benefit from the scheme find ways to lobby the government in pursuit of higher prices. Commercial farmers in Zimbabwe had mixed feelings about the whole issue of government control. On the one hand, the system guaranteed prices over which they had some influence, unlike market determined prices. On the other hand, farmers were seeing the Zimbabwean dollar's unofficial rate depreciate through the late 1980s, which would make their crops cheaper for the international markets, and fuel exports. However, because the grain was sold directly to the Grain Marketing Boards, the farmers were unable to exploit this avenue. Thus the commercial farmers were torn about continued government involvement. Communal farmers had less lobbying power and fewer marketing opportunities, due to having fewer resources, though represented by the National Farmers Association of Zimbabwe (NFAZ).

The marketing boards also created another inefficiency through their pricing systems: They paid out the same price for agricultural products, no matter where they were located. Commercial producers generally located themselves in central locations, near depots and collection points, whereas communal producers were scattered in many different places. This meant that the government was in effect subsidizing the farms in more remote areas, to compensate for the difference in transportation costs.[11]

One thing was certain: This policy didn't encourage efficiency. The pricing policies created distortions in the market that led to shortages, as well as huge inefficiencies in the market. Essentially, the marketing boards had no budget limits, as the national government was required to finance any deficits, even if it was due to poor management.[12] In fact, there was no reward for good work, or punishment for poor work. It was no surprise, then, that deficits were rising each year. Naturally those who benefited from the subsidies voiced concerns about the economic dislocations, but pro-market advocates (such as The World Bank) argued that cutting subsidies in inefficient programs would free up private capital expenditures.

With government deficits growing ever more rapidly, the World Bank put more pressure on Zimbabwe to move towards deregulation, and Zimbabwe responded that they would need aid from the World Bank to make the transition. The World Bank agreed to lend funds for this purpose, and reform appeared to be on its way.

Evaluating the Outcomes of the Economic Reforms

In 1990, the Zimbabwean government unveiled a new Economic Structural Adjustment Program (ESAP) in a report titled "Framework for Economic Reform 1991-95. It contained the typical features of a World Bank "rescue" strategy: (a) lowering the budget deficit; (b) trade liberalization, which meant expansion of free trade and devaluation of the Zimbabwean dollar; and (c) deregulating domestic markets by phasing out subsidies and eliminating price controls.[13] The World Bank gave $75 million in 1991, and an additional $50 million in 1994 to aid in this transition period.[14]

One of the main targets was to reduce the fiscal budget deficit from 10 percent of GDP in 1989-90 to 5 percent by 1994-95. Areas marked for cutting expenditures included the agricultural boards such as the GMB. ESAP also recommended firing government workers and increasing the citizen's share of the expense for health care and education.

The farmers opposed the agricultural reforms, because it meant they would not have government guarantees for crop prices. These crop prices typically exceeded the market price. However, the report argued that creating a freer market for agriculture would improve the conditions for these farmers. The argument, as summarized by a later World Bank report, was that "...rural decision-makers (could) allocate resources in line with their comparative advantages (which was) expected to improve incomes."[15] The Zimbabwean government claimed that up to 100,000 new jobs could be created in the formal sector annually after the full implementation of ESAP.[16]

One of the attractions of life before ESAP (as it is in any socialist regime) was employment security. Particularly for those workers who were employed in the government parastatals, generous wage hikes were common in the early 1990s, with the national government underwriting all excess expenditures.

Yet four years after the introduction of ESAP, it appeared that ESAP had made things worse for ordinary people. The ending of price controls meant that prices for ordinary foods such as maize had shot up by 235 percent in one year. Milk prices rose by 26 percent and soybeans jumped by 90 percent. By March 1993, the price of basic commodities had risen by 400 percent since 1990, while wages had increased by at most 20 percent during the same time. According to one survey, three quarters of the respondents had cut their food intake since the beginning of ESAP; many complained of dizziness, weakness, headaches and loss of weight. Households cut back on meat, fruit, eggs and chicken, and resorted to cheaper sources of calories like maize.[17] Employee benefits were cut as well. Over a third of all surveyed workers had had medical, tuition and housing benefits either cut or withdrawn. Formal job creation was not the promised 100,000 new jobs annually, but rather something closer to 4000-8000 jobs. As the drought receded in 1993, the economy did not pick up as expected. Angry bank, health and university workers staged strikes in late 1993, and 10,000 telecommunication and postal workers struck in early 1994.[18]

Table 4.1. Evolution of Zimbabwean Policies, Fiscal Years 1991-1995.

Year	Key event	Agricultural price policy.
1991	ESAP introduced. Severe drought begins.	• Phased elimination of controls on trade between smallholder areas.
1992	Severe drought	• Government continues to intervene in maize markets. • Price controls lifted on all but two fertilizers; government continues to manage imports through permits. • Subsidies to marketing boards grow.
1993	ESAP reforms	• Grain Marketing Board monopoly seller status restricted to large mills. • High official producer price announced to promote planting • Maize meal subsidies removed. • Subsidies to marketing boards fall by 83%. • Consumer prices decontrolled. • Cotton marketing board eliminated.
1994	Second drought begins	• Grain Marketing Board monopoly status eliminated. • Exporters allowed to retain 100% of export earnings.
1995	Second drought	• All fertilizer price controls ended. • Subsidies to marketing boards eliminated.

The information above was adapted from Alwang, Jeffrey et. al. in "Why Has Poverty Increased in Zimbabwe?" World Bank: March 2002, in Table 1.Evolution of Zimbabwean Policies, Fiscal Years 1990-1996.

The focus of ESAP had been to wean the government off a habit of spending more than it earned, but here the harsh treatment failed. Despite assurances to the World Bank that it would quit its subsidies, by the late 1990s the government was back to subsidizing the grain marketing board (GMB), spending increasingly worthless Zimbabwean dollars. The government's response to this crisis was to print money even faster, setting the stage for hyperinflation.

Through the 1980s real GDP growth in Zimbabwe had averaged 5.2 percent, yet during the years of ESAP in the 1990s, real GDP growth had slowed to 2.9 percent. By 1999 the economy was in a mild recession, with real GDP growth at –0.7 percent, down from 2.9 percent the year earlier. It was clear that ESAP was far from a success, but it would be unfair to blame the slowdown in economic growth because of it. In many ways, ESAP simply unveiled the structural imbalances that had been present in the economy for the past decade. With or without ESAP, Zimbabwe had been on a questionable course for some time, spending far more than it received in tax revenue.

Was the 2001/02 Drought to Blame For Zimbabwe's Collapse?

In its annual Article IV (June 2003) report, The World Bank provided an extensive overview of Zimbabwe's problems and presented recommendations. At the top of the list of problems was the 2001-02 African drought. This was convenient for President Mugabe, given that the weather is beyond the government's control. Despite the fact that Zimbabwe's missteps cost it World Bank voting rights and borrowing privileges, the Bank's Executive Director for Zimbabwe argued the country deserved another chance, stating that the drought was the "worst in five decades."[19] The source of this information in the Bank's report was the World Food Program. However, an official news release from the World Food Program called the 2001-02 drought in Zimbabwe "the longest in 20 years."[20]

The Foreign Agricultural Service, an arm of the United States Department of Agriculture, reported in February of 2002 an even less alarming story. Until mid-December of 2001, the report stated that "widespread above normal rainfall and seasonable temperatures were very favorable for recently planted summer crops (in Zimbabwe)."[21] It acknowledged that a developing drought was threatening summer crop yields across Zimbabwe in the spring of 2002. This analysis was based on data obtained from four rainfall stations, based in the area of Gokwe, Gweru, Harare Kutsage, and Masvingo.

In the spring of 2002, The United Nations' Food and Agricultural Organization (FAO), in conjunction with the World Food Program (WFP), led an assessment mission in Zimbabwe, aimed at detailing the food production, the level of the drought and the emergency food requirements. During this time, the FAO/WFP staff held meetings in Harare with government and farming representatives, including the Commercial Farmers Union, Zimbabwe Farmers Union and the

Indigenous Commercial Farmers Union. The FAO/WFP also made field visits to 24 districts and spoke with farmers, laborers, traders, project workers and government officials. The results of their mission were laid out in a May 29, 2002 report, which concluded that a drought had lasted from January 2002 to early April 2002. There were virtually no crops for the field workers to inspect and the "major cause" of this was listed to be the drought.[22] However, the report noted that the dry spell "primarily affected the southern districts, which received less than 30 percent of the long-term mean for the months of January and February." Most areas to the north "received rainfall in the average range" in the fall, and in the 75 percent range in the spring.[23] Yet maize, the staple food of Zimbabweans is primarily grown in the northernmost districts of Mashonaland West, Mashonaland Central and Mashonaland East.[24]

The drought therefore applied not to the entire 2001/02 crop year as was implied by the World Bank report, but rather to a three-month dry spell in the spring of 2002. Considering this three-month dry spell in isolation, it was indeed one of the longest in the past 20 years, and also ranks fifth in drought severity for these three months since 1900. However, the FAO/WFP report also says that this analysis was carried out "using a few selected stations in the eight provinces of Zimbabwe."[25] There are eighty rainfall stations in Zimbabwe, so there is obviously some room for error in this analysis.

The 2001/2002 Drought: A Closer Analysis

A more nuanced view of the drought can be gained by examining Zimbabwe's official rainfall data, which was obtained by this author with permission from Zimbabwe's Department of Meteorology. These primary data included individual data on 80 rainfall stations, reported on a month-to-month basis, over a period of up to 50 years. The data were aggregated and averaged for use in the analysis below. Only 48 stations logged data back as far as 50 years.

Using data from 80 rainfall stations for the period 1981-2003 (1980/81 corresponds to 1981 on the graph, for example), Figure 4.1 below shows that the economy once hinged on rainfall. From 1980 to 1999 the correlation between real GDP growth and rainfall was calculated to be 0.69. In other words, 69 percent of GDP growth was correlated with rainfall, giving an excellent indication of just

Figure 4.1. Rainfall vs. GDP in Zimbabwe: 1981-2003

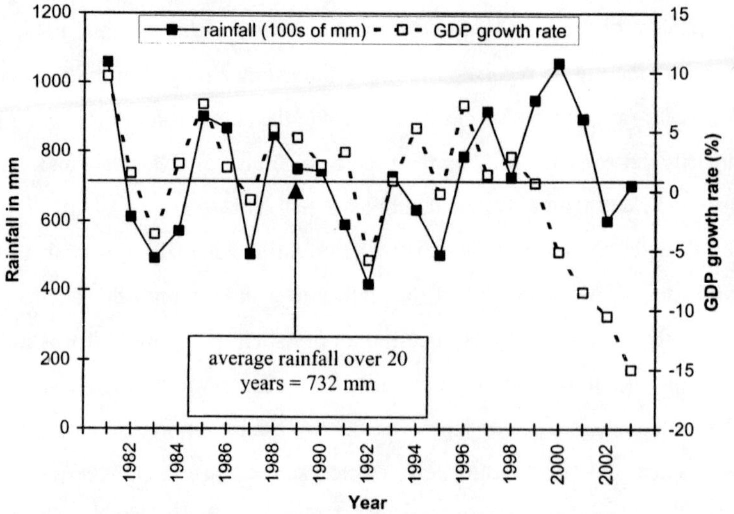

Source: Department of Meteorology, Zimbabwe and Economist Intelligence Unit, various years.

how important the agricultural sector was in driving the economy. With the economy sputtering at –0.7 percent growth in 1999, the link between GDP and rainfall then sharply disconnected in the year 2000, the year of the land reforms. GDP growth plunged downward, even as rainfall returned to above normal levels. The graph shows a clear break from the past 20-year pattern, indicating the serious collapse in the agricultural sector's production levels. Yet during 2003, stories continued to persist from relief organizations about a continuing drought despite the restoration of normal rainfall patterns.[26]

Using the data from Table 4.2, one can infer a different conclusion than the World Bank regarding the 2001/02 crop season. The amount of rainfall during this time was just 22% below the 50-year average. By assuming rainfall to be normally distributed over 50 years[a], one can infer the probability of Zimbabwe receiving a given amount of rainfall or less. For example, as Table 4.2 shows below, the 91/92 drought of 425 mm of rain was in the 2.8th percentile, indicating that in a random year, rainfall exceeds this measurement 97.2 percent of the time. For the 2001/2002 season, the cumulative rainfall fell in the 21st percentile, indicating that about one out of every five growing seasons has this level of rainfall or less. This puts some perspective on the "worst drought in 50 years" comment. By ranking cumulative rainfall over the past 50 years from lowest to highest, the 2001/02 growing season comes in 13th place.

To be sure, the weather patterns during 2001/02 were far from normal. Weather extremes, from very soggy in late 2001 to extremely dry in the early part of 2002, hurt crop yields. An investigation into the average drop in rainfall for the months of January through March for 48 rainfall stations[b] showed that there was indeed a very severe drought for those three months. The average rainfall during this time was found to be 58 percent below the average.

There is indeed no doubt that the 3-month drought caused devastation for communal farmers. However, to put primary blame on the drought for the sudden drop in overall agricultural production, as the FAO/WFP and the World Bank do, misses a key point. Zimbabwe differs significantly from other African countries that suffered through the same drought. The reason is that it possessed large dams and well-engineered irrigation systems for its commercial farming regions. Because of the early and large amount of rainfall in late 2001, dams throughout Zimbabwe were reported as full, with enough water to last through the next rainy season.[27]

---

[a] A plotting of the rainfall data over 50 years shows this to be a reasonable assumption.
[b] Only 48 rainfall stations had records going back 50 years.

Table 4.2
The Top Fifteen Droughts in Zimbabwe Over 50 Years

Rank	Year	Rainfall	Percentile	Percent below/above average
1	91/92	425.1	2.8%	-77.4
2	72/73	488.0	6.1%	-54.6
3	94/95	491.6	6.4%	-53.4
4	82/83	502.3	7.2%	-50.1
5	67/68	502.9	7.2%	-50.0
6	86/87	516.6	8.4%	-46.0
7	63/64	544.7	11.2%	-38.5
8	81/82	573.5	14.7%	-31.5
9	83/84	577.6	15.3%	-30.6
10	90/91	586.5	16.5%	-28.6
11	93/94	615.9	21.1%	-22.5
12	64/65	616.8	21.2%	-22.3
13	**2001/2002**	**616.9**	**21.2%**	**-22.2**
14	59/60	617.4	21.3%	-22.2
15	78/79	636.5	24.7%	-18.5

Source: Primary data from 48 rainfall stations, reported directly to the Department of Meteorology, Zimbabwe. Calculations by author. (The average rainfall for the past 50 years was 754.7 mm.)

Andrew Natsios, an administrator for the U.S Agency for International Development, noted in an August 20, 2002 foreign press briefing on Zimbabwe that, "There is water available, even if there's a second-year drought, to grow a crop, but the crops aren't being planted because the commercial farmers and farm workers have been evicted by the government. We have urged them to reconsider their expropriation of these farms at a time when that really was the insurance policy for people to survive in a severe drought."[28]

Sharp Changes in Agricultural Production

The simultaneous collapse of the both the communal and commercial agricultural sectors underscored the two key functions that crops perform for Zimbabwe's economy. First, they provide millions of citizens a means to sustain themselves and over half of the jobs. Second, the crops trade for hard currency, through the sales of everything from flowers to tobacco. This hard currency gives Zimbabwe a means to purchase imports of everything from fertilizer and seeds to cars and gasoline. Thus, both of these functions thus serve as the crucial backbone for the Zimbabwe economy, and help explain the economic crash of Zimbabwe.

The impact of the drought on commercial versus communal farms

Communal farmers plant most of the maize, with the goal of providing daily subsistence for themselves and their families. It serves as Zimbabwe's most important staple food. However, prior to 2000, about 4,000 commercial farmers grew 38 percent of all maize production in Zimbabwe, selling the extra crops for profit both at home and abroad, as seen in Table 4.3 below.

The communal farms tend to be in drier areas. This makes them particularly vulnerable to droughts. The 2001/02 drought hit the communal farmers hard, with communal maize production dropping by a stunning two-thirds, from 1.091 million tons in 2000/01 to only 315,000 tons the following year.

This would have been the key time for Zimbabwe's insurance policy- its irrigated commercial farm system- to greatly ameliorate the harm of the drought, by providing the hard currency for seeds for the following year, and food for the present. In the absence of land seizures, Zimbabwe would have simply exported very little of its maize and used the majority of it to feed its people. The drought would have registered as a "tough year" but hardly a catastrophe, as the following year brought restorative rains. The commercial farms' abilities to weather severe droughts is demonstrated by examining the changes in maize yield for communal vs. commercial farmers, on a per hectare basis. As Table 4.3 shows below, during the 2001-02 drought the yield for maize per hectare only dropped 16% for commercial farmers whose land had not yet been seized, from 4.28 to 3.70 tons per hectare. Communal farmers' yield, on the other hand, fell precipitously by nearly three-fourths of the previous year's production levels.

The drought reduced communal farms to only 7% of the productivity of commercial farms by the end of 2002, whereas they had been 28% as efficient in 1999/2000. Another way of putting this is that in the 1999/2000 crop year, 1 hectare of commercially farmed land produced the same as 3.6 hectares of communally farmed land. Two years later, the ratio was 1 to 15, even using the evicted commercial farmland. With such a stunning drop in production levels, combined with the hundreds of thousands of hectares lying idle, it was no wonder Zimbabwe, once called Africa's breadbasket, was now a basket case.

Table 4.3. Differences in Yields and Production between Communal and Commercial Farms, for Maize Production, 1999-2002.

Yield (tons per hectare)	1999/2000	2000/2001	2001/2002
Communal farms	1.13	0.96	0.25
Commercial farms	4.05	4.28	3.70
Communal/commercial production.	0.279	0.224	0.068
Production (1,000s of tons			
Communal farms	1,338	1,091	315
Commercial farms	810	385	185

Data came from Statistical Appendix, Table 3, in the June 2003 IMF report, which used information from official government agencies in Zimbabwe.

The conversion from commercial to communal farming

Not only were the communal farms becoming sharply less productive during the drought, there were also far more of them, as the government converted commercial farms to communal ones. In 1999/2000 the commercial farmers planted 200,000 hectares of farmland; in 2000/01 it was 90,000 hectares, and by 2001/02 it was only 50,000 hectares, as seen in Figure 4.2.[29]

The land has been redistributed to peasant farmers, urban bureaucrats and members of ZANU-PF's political elite. Roughly 120,000 new communal farmers settled on these lands as of 2002, even as 825,000 commercial farm workers (primarily black) lost their jobs.[30] One BBC report noted that the political elite who "travel down in luxury 4-wheel drive vehicles to inspect their newly acquired farms over weekends are known as the 'weekend' farmers." Critics of the Mugabe regime cynically noted that the land reform program was simply an inexpensive way for Mugabe to buy political patronage and remain in power.[31] Of the 4,500 white commercial farmers forced off the land through 2003, only 120 ultimately were paid any compensation. These were the ones who did not appeal to the courts against the loss of their farms.

Figure 4.2. Changes in area planted for maize, commercial farms.

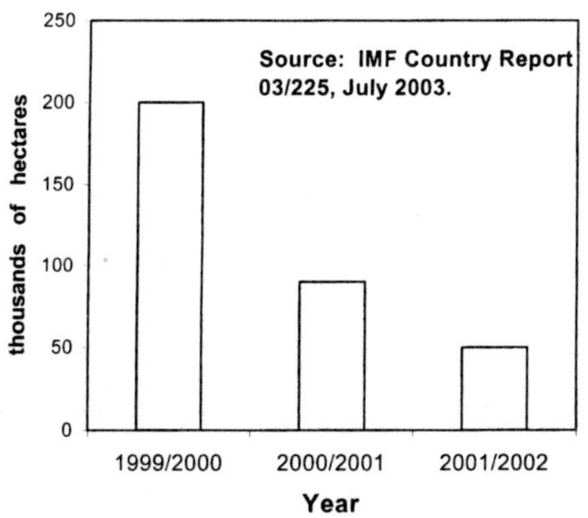

Unfortunately, without a plan for redistribution or access to property titles, half of the vacated farms were left unclaimed and unused. As a result, the rural land market collapsed. New farmers do not have titles to the land. In addition, the government's shortfall of hard currency meant that the new farmers also have no money for seeds, and no collateral for capital investments such as tractors and tilling equipment. They lease the land from the government on a year-to-year basis, at the behest of the government, and there are no plans in place for these persons to buy these farms. In most cases the farm acquisitions are subject to litigation, and few banking organizations are willing to provide credit.[32]

With the absence of property rights, Zimbabwe's advanced system of commercial farming quickly liquidated. Evicted farmers dug up, sold or took the irrigation pipes; some ZANU-PF supporters even melted pipes down to sell as coffin handles or scrap metal.[33] Sophisticated farming equipment was looted, set on fire or stolen by marauding groups. To make matters worse, the Grain Marketing Board (GMB), run by the Zimbabwe government, delivered seeds late in 2001, and many communal farmers criticized it because their maize crops did not receive a basal fertilizer dressing, which is important for root growth. Without it, maize is very susceptible to droughts.[34] In addition, the people who replaced the commercial farmers lacked the knowledge of running a commercial farm, and many farms were simply left fallow or the wrong types of inputs were used.

The poverty trap

Hundreds of thousands of small-scale farmers have now been "plunged into a poverty trap by the government."[35] Joseph Made, Zimbabwe's Minister of Lands, Agriculture and Rural Resettlement finally admitted that the land reform program was "haphazard", although plans still were in place to resettle tens of thousands of black Zimbabweans, and continue the program.[36] The following description from a 2003 *National Geographic* article gives a journalist's vivid picture of the catastrophic effect of the land reform movement on the Devillefarm in the Mazowe Valley:

> After the winter wheat came in, there would be virtually no more activity on the farm, and the hundred workers would be out of jobs. The 45 acres of citrus trees were wilting and would soon die — the irrigation piping on which their health depended had been dug up and sold by the major's men. The greenhouses where the Selbys grew roses for export to the Netherlands were nothing now but a torn skin of plastic, flapping in the breeze against the exposed skeletons of wooden struts. The swimming pool was dark with rotting leaves; the clay tennis court had sprouted a quiff of elephant grass. Delvillewood Farm was rapidly returning to the bush.[37]

In addition, the seizure had forced the closure of their bakery, which had served 15,000 people, and their butchery and trading store. By 2003, over 1 million workers related to farm activity had been displaced, with few places to go.

Where *do* they go? Some illegally cross the border into South Africa, working menial jobs, such as street vendors, or in tenement-style sewing factories. South African officials say that the country deports at least 2,500 Zimbabweans each month, on the train and in trucks. One despairing 18-year-old passenger named Xolani Masuko had been deported twice in less than a year, saying, "It's like to die. 'I don't have money. I don't have food. I don't have everything. The whole family died of H.I.V."[38] Others find themselves in places like Rock Haven refugee camp in Zimbabwe, which has tents housing about 200 farm workers who formerly worked at the Chipesa Farm, owned by Iain Kay. Kay had openly opposed Mugabe prior to elections. One of the refugees, James Sani, told the story:

> "One day the war vets and party youth arrived on our farm and said it belonged to them now. They put a gun to Iain Kay. The vets beat us with iron bars and axes, and they looted our property and chased us away."

Another Chipesa worker, Armando Serima spoke up as well:

> "They called us muvengi, enemy, because they said we supported the opposition party. We hid in the bush eating roots and leaves and begging food from other farm workers at night, until Mr. Kay came and found us hiding there in the mountains just when we were about to die of hunger, and he brought us here. So we have nothing. I was born at the farm, grew up at the farm, and went to school on the farm, worked for the past eight years on the farm. My father died on the farm. All we know is farming. That's what we want to do again."[39]

Declines in revenues

Zimbabwe's government now faced two enormous and pressing problems as its commercial sector disappeared. First, it was apparent that with the precipitous drop in maize production, its citizens would no longer be able to feed themselves. Second, its most lucrative cash crops were no longer providing sufficient foreign exchange. Zimbabwe's decline in cash crops badly hurt the government's coffers, which depend on hard currency. From 1999 to 2000, commercial farm revenue dropped in staggering fashion, from 877 million U.S. dollars to just 247 million U.S. dollars.

As seen in Figure 4.3 below, tobacco was the most important cash crop, supplying 70 percent of all foreign exchange. It had production levels fall by two-thirds by 2003. Tobacco is an especially attractive crop because its global commodity prices are relatively stable, as is its ability to survive highly variable weather conditions. It is also less perishable than other crops, and is easier to deliver and stow.[40]

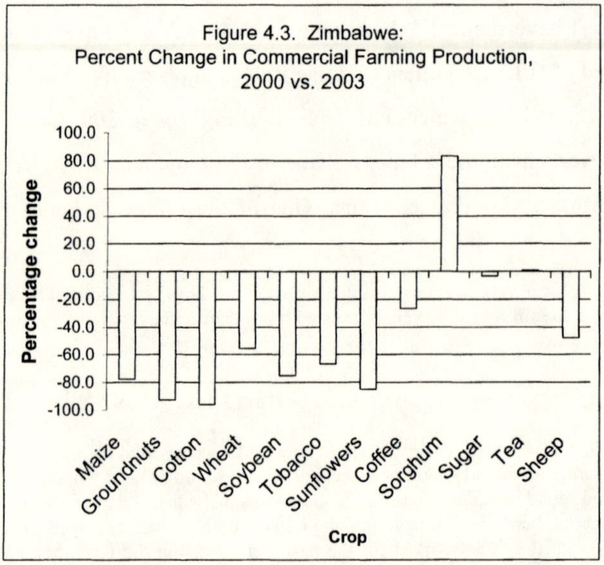

Cotton, an important export crop and a source of foreign exchange as well, crashed by 96% in three years. Sugarcane production was the only important cash crop to survive relatively unscathed, with levels falling by only 3 percent. A rare bright spot was drought-resistant sorghum, with production levels rising by a dramatic 83%, but only 5,000 hectares was planted.[41] (A more detailed breakdown of these statistics is seen in Table 4.4.) The higher value crops such as tobacco were harder hit than the lower value crops, which resulted in critical shortages of foreign exchange. Farmers need 10-15% of the foreign exchange that they earn each year to service their own needs, such as imports of farm inputs like gasoline and machine parts.

In normal years, the balance of the foreign exchange from the agricultural sector provided between 40-45% of the total foreign exchange for the country; of this percentage, around 80% originates from the commercial farm sub-sector.[42] Clearly this was a debilitating loss of revenue for the Mugabe government, and the economy at large. The lack of hard currency caused by the collapse of the commercial farming sector meant that the government had little money to spend on important agricultural inputs for the communal farmers, such as fertilizer. In addition, the deficit-ridden GMB was unable to guarantee a pre-planting price for maize, which made farmers reluctant to produce a crop that probably would have a very low return. Price controls on fertilizer created shortages, as companies were reluctant to deliver the input at a loss. Late payments by the GMB the previous year also stymied farmers' initiative to grow maize.[43] As a result, thousands of hectares remained fallow after 2000, adding to the collapse of production caused by the drought and the land reforms.

The spread to manufacturing

The damage done to the agricultural sector spread quickly to the manufacturing sector. About 60% of manufacturing firms are dependent upon agriculture for either raw materials for processing, or as a market for manufactured agricultural inputs (e.g. fertilizer). Because of the drop in agricultural output, capacity utilization of manufacturing now averages 50 percent, according to OECD estimates.[44] In addition, industrial production declined by 10.5 percent in 2001 and an estimated 17.5 percent in 2002. The report also notes that "Besides declines in food processing and beverages companies, the machinery and transport sectors have suffered from the weaker demand by commercial farmers as a result of the land reform process and the government's handling of property rights.

Table 4.4

ESTIMATED TOTAL PRODUCTION LARGE SCALE COMMERCIAL SECTOR (1000's of metric tons)

	1998	1999	2000	2001	2002	2003	Percent change, 2000-2003
Maize	521.01	648.00	810.00	384.80	185.40	180.00	
Percent change		**24.37**	**25.00**	**-52.49**	**-51.82**	**-2.91**	**-77.78**
Groundnuts	2.81	2.00	4.20	5.00	1.80	0.30	
Percent change		**-28.88**	**110.00**	**19.05**	**-64.00**	**-83.33**	**-92.86**
Cotton	76.54	61.10	52.80	38.28	15.89	2.11	
Percent change		**-20.17**	**-13.58**	**-27.51**	**-58.49**	**-86.74**	**-96.01**
Wheat	270.00	281.25	225.00	282.60	152.50	100.00	
Percent change		**4.17**	**-20.00**	**25.60**	**-46.04**	**-34.43**	**-55.56**
Soybean	108.00	122.20	145.00	162.50	64.75	36.00	
Percent change		**13.15**	**18.66**	**12.07**	**-60.15**	**-44.40**	**-75.17**
Tobacco	213.12	191.51	232.25	197.20	155.95	76.87	
Percent change		**-10.14**	**21.27**	**-15.09**	**-20.92**	**-50.71**	**-66.90**
Sunflowers	1.23	1.50	3.00	2.00	0.60	0.45	
Percent change		**21.75**	**100.00**	**-33.33**	**-70.00**	**-25.00**	**-85.00**
Coffee	10.00	10.00	7.50	7.21	8.80	5.50	
Percent change		**0.00**	**-25.00**	**-3.84**	**22.02**	**-37.50**	**-26.67**
Sorghum	22.61	12.00	18.00	18.55	15.00	33.00	
Percent change		**-46.94**	**50.00**	**3.06**	**-19.14**	**120.00**	**83.33**
Sugar	570.13	570.00	537.49	514.93	580.50	520.00	
Percent change		**-0.02**	**-5.70**	**-4.20**	**12.73**	**-10.42**	**-3.25**
Tea	18.20	18.53	21.82	21.73	22.50	22.00	
Percent change		**1.82**	**17.74**	**-0.43**	**3.57**	**-2.22**	**0.83**
Sheep	0.27	0.30	0.29	0.30	0.30	0.15	
Percent change		**9.36**	**-3.03**	**4.17**	**0.00**	**-50.00**	**-47.92**
Horticulture	54.86	64.66	67.40	77.54	81.28	55.30	
Percent change		**17.87**	**4.24**	**15.06**	**4.82**	**-31.96**	**-17.95**

Source: Calculations made using data from the Economics Department, Commercial Farmers Union, provided October 2003.

The downward spiral has the potential to get worse each year, as crops are not adequately fertilized, which results in lower yields, and even less money for fertilizer the following year.

Dead capital: The loss in farmland wealth

As Hernando de Soto would have predicted, banks lost millions of dollars in loans as white farmers left, leaving no collateral in return.[45] By taking the total revenue from commercial production obtained from The Commercial Farmers Union, the loss in wealth from 1997 to 2003 can be imputed, as explained in Table 4.5 below. The Figures 4.4 and 4.5 below illustrate the numbers. By 2003, nearly 7 billion US dollars in wealth had vanished from the agricultural sector, and what was left was dead capital, unable to generate new economic activity because the land was not titled. There is a telling statistic that reflects the lack of leveraging ability by farmers today. Prior to 1997, an average of 1,600 tractors were sold per year; in 2002 total sales for the entire country had fallen to eight tractors.[46]

Table 4.5. The Loss in Agricultural Revenue, and Wealth from Commercial Farmland 1997-2003.

	1997	1998	1999	2000	2001	2002	2003
Total commercial agricultural revenue, in millions of Zimbabwean dollars	13,300	21,184	33,603	48,933	102,843	249,239	524,560
Parallel exchange rate (Z$ to US$)	11.9	21.4	38.3	200.0	410.0	1,100.0	1,800.0
Total, in millions of U.S. dollars	1,118.6	989.4	877.1	244.7	250.8	226.6	291.4
Imputed Value of Commercial Farmland, billions of US $	9.38	8.30	7.36	2.05	2.10	1.90	2.44
Cumulative loss, US billions of $		**-1.08**	**-2.02**	**-7.33**	**-7.28**	**-7.48**	**-6.94**

Source: CFU, IMF, and author calculations.

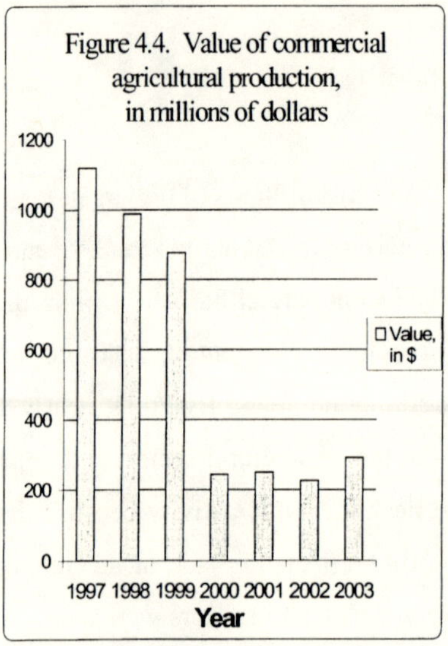

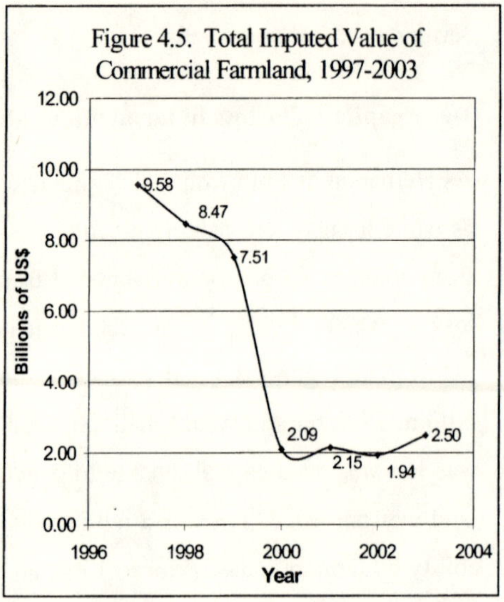

<u>*Note on calculation for Table 4.5 and Figure 4.5*</u>: The total value of commercial farmland is difficult to calculate, given the fast-changing environment of high inflation and parallel exchange rates. An admittedly crude estimate was imputed using the available information. First, it is known that in 1997 there were 11.3 million hectares of commercial farmland. The average selling price in that year was Z$9,883 per hectare (Rugube, 2001, p. 17.)

There was slightly above average rainfall this year, making it a good representative year for typical agricultural revenue. Therefore, the total value of farmland in that year was approximately Z$111.678 billion, or US$9.384 billion, using the parallel exchange rate in that year of 11.9Z$=1 US$. According the CFU, commercial farmers earned US$1.119 billion in revenue in 1997. That is a return of 11.92 percent. Using that return, the approximate value of commercial farmland in succeeding years was imputed by dividing the value of agricultural production by 0.1192. Clearly the significant drop was due in large part to the land seizures.

Chapter 5. The Foreign Exchange and Monetary Crises

Where Did the Hard Currency Go?

As we have seen, the huge drop in agricultural production led to a crash in exports, which severely impacted Zimbabwe's holdings of hard currency. The Zimbabwean government and businesspeople depend upon foreign exchange for many needs. Farmers need chemicals, fuel, and fertilizer; mining operations require tools, fuel and spare parts; and the government needs hard currency for many essentials, including imported electricity and payment of loans from the international community.

In addition, within a year after the land seizures, in early 2001, Zimbabwe was beginning to feel the effects of the world's increasing lack of confidence in its future. The poor crop yields and errant government policies signaled a highly questionable future to foreign investors. As can be seen in Figure 5.1, the parallel exchange rate, or unofficial "street" price, was essentially equivalent to the official exchange rate right up to January of 2001. This rate was 55 Z$ to 1 US$.

However, the two sharply diverged soon after, with the government making no effort to readjust official exchange rates in line with supply and demand. As the number of land seizures increased, perceptions about law and order (concordant with reality) changed; lack of confidence in the government's policies sharply increased. To tourists, Zimbabwe appeared to no longer be a welcoming place, and there were big drops in visits to popular areas like Victoria Falls. United

States dollars, highly undervalued at the official rate, predictably became in extremely short supply, making the parallel markets take on increasing significance. The Mugabe government's refusal to take this seriously (by devaluing the Zimbabwe dollar) would be one of the most significant economic mistakes of the regime, causing ordinary law-abiding Zimbabweans to become surreptitious traders dealing in underground markets.

The Costs of Parallel Exchange Rates

Parallel exchange rates develop as authorities vainly try to impose restrictions on access to foreign currency in an effort to maintain an overvalued exchange rate. The government has an incentive to maintain the rate, as it keeps imports cheaper. It also makes it less expensive to meet foreign debt obligations. However, the government is simply borrowing time, as the rest of the world's notional value of the currency sharply diverges from the government's wishful thinking. When parallel exchange rates widely diverge from official ones, it often turns law-abiding citizens into cheats and law-breakers.

For example, under conditions like Zimbabwe's since 2000, traders have a large incentive to misrepresent their shipments on their invoices. Both "under-invoicing" and "over-invoicing" are likely to happen under these circumstances. Under-invoicing occurs when exporters under-report the value of their sales. They do this by setting up foreign subsidiaries, and letting foreigners pay hard currency to these companies. So even less hard currency enters the country. Importers, on the other hand, have an incentive to over-value their imports, to get more domestic currency from the government. Both types of misrepresentations can result in greater profits for traders. The government now must devote more resources towards finding and punishing these lawbreakers, leaving less money for other more productive uses. In addition, from a macro-economic standpoint, the revenue collected by government drops even further.[47]

In sum, these parallel markets attempt to hide the rising cost of imports through an artificial exchange rate. As is always the case, the cost surfaces somewhere else, albeit in a hidden form. In this case, the cost is the enormous amount of wasted time devoted to simply finding, hiding, and securing hard currency- activity that has no net productive use to society.

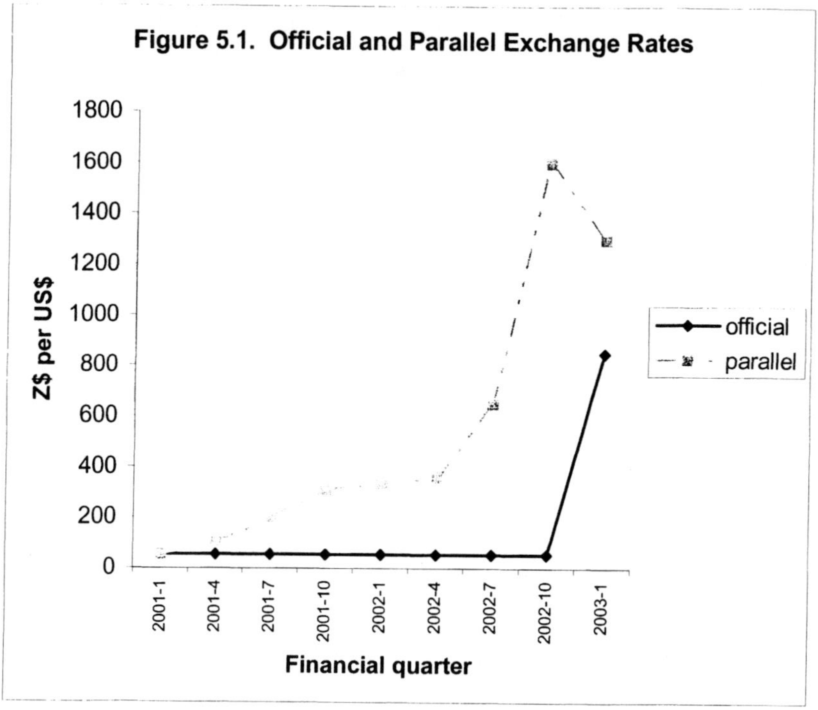

Source: June 2003 IMF Report 03/225. p. 86.

Further downward pressures

As mentioned earlier, the sharp drop-offs in agricultural production led to a tremendous drop in exports, which had provided a crucial flow of hard currency. Tobacco alone had accounted for 70 percent of Zimbabwe's exports.[48] In addition, runaway inflation by 2002 made it more and more difficult for Zimbabweans to purchase imported goods. The result was a dramatic turn of events for what was once one of the few countries in sub-Saharan Africa that exported more than it imported. The current account, which previously had been solidly in the black, swung suddenly into the red, indicating the vast number of imports Zimbabwe now required just to stay afloat, as seen in Figure 5.2.

Because Zimbabwe failed to meet its foreign payment obligations, The IMF declared in September 2001 that the country was ineligible to use IMF resources. By mid-June 2002, the total external payments arrears were US$1.03 billion.[49] Since Zimbabwe imports electricity, and depends upon foreign exchange, it was having difficulty coming up with the currency to pay for the power. As a result, a utility company in Mozambique, owed US$6.67 million, decided to reduce electricity supplies due to non-payment. Eskom of South Africa owed US$5.07 million, decided to make Zimbabwe an interruptible customer, which means supplies can be reduced at any time. Even the national airline, Air Zimbabwe was in trouble. It owed US$22.6 million to the World Bank, or it risked having its aircraft impounded.[50]

The government's response: tightening price controls

In November of 2002, the Zimbabwe government responded to the accelerating inflation by tightening price controls. Price controls had initially only been imposed on a select number of consumer goods in October of 2001, but rising commodity prices through the year led to the government attempting to exert ever more control over pricing. The controls again masked the true nature of the problem, as shortages predictably increased, as did black market exchanges, where the prices were even higher.[51] In early May of 2003, however, the government announced it was easing price controls on some products, although food staples continued to be controlled.[52] Meanwhile, foreign exchange traders were reporting virtually no trading activity at the official rates.

The shortages of hard currency and products took their toll. One story told in *The Economist* related how a Zimbabwean zipper maker lost an $8,000 order because in 2001 it didn't have $100 in hard currency for the imported metal studs needed to make the zippers. The newsmagazine reported that rich individuals began putting their assets into things like jewelry and diamonds, things that could be easily taken out of the country, as opposed to houses or land that might be seized.[53]

Currency meltdown

In October 2001, international airlines no longer accepted Z$ for flights, as they were already sitting on mountains of increasingly worthless Zimbabwean currency. With the parallel exchange rate now trading 300 Zimbabwean dollars for 1 U.S. dollar, airlines still were forced to go through official foreign exchanges, giving them 55 Z$ to 1 US dollar. (They could not trade in the reverse direction.) In an economy with inflation sharply rising, airlines needed more money for fuel, and spare parts, but the fixed exchange rate was preventing them

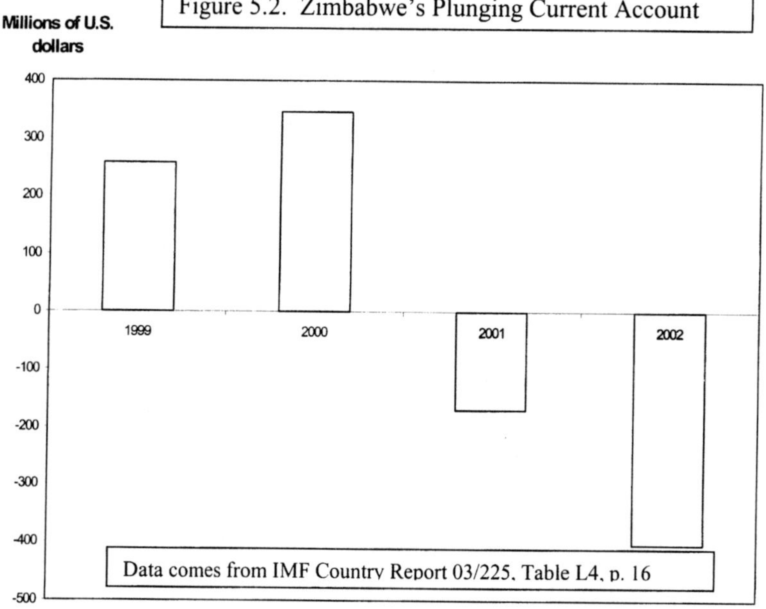
Figure 5.2. Zimbabwe's Plunging Current Account

from acquiring it. Local currency was no longer accepted for international calls either.[54]

The government tried to control the deteriorating situation. In January 2002, it imposed strict penalties of bank trading in foreign currency outside official foreign exchange markets. Foreign exchange outlets were forbidden to keep more than $100,000 in cash. They were accused of being the main channel for leaking foreign exchange to parallel markets. Official licensing costs were increased from $50,000 to $150,000, which the government claimed would "streamline the system."[55] Of course, the real reason was to sharply curtail parallel markets.

To attempt to capture more hard currency, the Central Bank demanded that forty percent of export receipts in hard currency needed to be surrendered to the Central Bank, at the official exchange rate of 55 Z$ to 1 US$. Meanwhile, government officials parlayed those dollars into Zimbabwean dollars at a far higher rate of exchange. The foreign exchange crisis continued to mount. By late January 2002, the parallel exchange rate was 330 Z$ to 1 US$. Hundreds of millions of dollars of stock were sold by foreigners, and the Zimbabwean stock exchange plummeted.[56] Finally in early 2003, facing a severe shortage of dollars, the government raised the official trading price to 824Z$ to 1 US dollar. By this time the parallel exchange rate was trading at around Z$1,400 to 1, making little difference.[57]

Like a sandcastle being lashed by an increasing tide, the Zimbabwean economy continued to crumble. In response, the government tightened its grip, but its overly tight grasp only succeeded in creating further cracks. The Bureaux de Changes were closed across the country at the end of December 2002, which resulted in further losses in business confidence. In addition, exporters were told they now had to rescind 50% of their earnings in hard currency to the Central Bank of Zimbabwe. This further "dampened market sentiment," according to a report by Intermarket Holding. The central bank reported that this was because estimates showed that by this time, 80 percent of foreign exchange transactions were taking place on the parallel market.[58]

These actions made little difference to the growing crisis. In fact, they made it worse. *The Financial Gazette* in January of 2003 reported that the new rules resulted in foreign exchange inflows plunging by 70%. In keeping with the earlier hypothesis about under-invoicing, the farmers may have been hiding their export earnings, as inflows did not even rise significantly during the tobacco-marketing season, which normally boosts Zimbabwe's hard cash earnings.[59]

Analysts interviewed by the paper said that it was clear from the Reserve Bank's own statistics that new regulations had failed to stamp out the parallel market. The improvement in hard currency inflows as a result of domestic trading was only slight after the Bureaux de Change closures.[60] Clearly the confidence in Zimbabwe's economy was continuing to plunge, with very few buyers of Zimbabwean dollars. As a result, the parallel market rate was more than 20 times the 55 to 1 rate. Zimbabwean dollars were now trading for 1,500 to $1.

Zimbabwe's total demand for hard currency now far exceeded the supply. For the period April 2002 to March 2003 it amounted to US $1.14 billion, a long way from the expected inflows of only US $486.4 million, according to a Ministry of Finance report.[61] The resulting deficit of US $660 million was reflected in critical shortages of essential inputs. Zimbabwe's payments on loans to The World Bank, already overdue, increased even further its payment arrears.

The Minister of Finance, Dr Simba Makoni, in a document entitled "Memorandum on Foreign Currency Position by the Minister of Finance and Economic Development", stated:

> "Zimbabwe's foreign currency situation remains critical, largely as a result of poor export performance coupled with the drying up of international balance of payments support. The country has no usable foreign exchange reserves and this has adversely affected the capacity to procure critical imports such as drugs, fuel, electricity and raw materials. This has been compounded by the need to import edible grain."[62]

It didn't seem like it could get much worse, but it did. By May of 2003, Zimbabwe's central bank ran out of foreign exchange to import the special paper and ink used to print currency.[63] It now had no way to finance its runaway deficits, although this may have been a blessing in disguise. By not being able to meet the "excess demand" for currency, the forced clampdown on the money supply should have slowed inflation. But not for long, as the government invented a new form of money printed on another paper, which it called a "bank note". Still its gross reserves were dropping to dangerously low levels. It had few places to turn, but one of those places was underground.

Wealth in Mining Operations

Like many African countries, Zimbabwe is rich in mineral resources, with more than thirty different minerals mined from the ground.[64] The minerals include gold, platinum, nickel, copper, coal, ferrochromium, lithium crystals, cobalt and granite.[65] Gold has long been the most important, spinning off one-fourth of all the mineral production revenue, and generating $273 million in hard currency in 1999.[66] With 90 percent of tobacco farmers gone from their properties, gold sales became the primary source of hard currency. Yet gold production began to decline as well.

In 1999 Zimbabwe produced 27.7 tons; four years later it had fallen by nearly half, to 15.2 tons.[67] Zimbabwe dropped from the third biggest gold producer on the African continent (after South Africa and Ghana) in 1999, to eighth largest in 2003.[68] Revenue from gold fell to only $153 million in 2001. By 2003, twelve fully productive gold mines had closed, and new projects were put on hold, as economic woes in Zimbabwe continued to mount, as seen in Figure 5.3 on the next page. Gross reserves (measured in U.S. dollars) held by the government dropped from nearly 500 million U.S. dollars to less than 200 million dollars, in just three years.

Figure 5.3. Total Gross Reserves held by Zimbabwean Government, 1998-2002 in millions of U.S dollars; end of period.

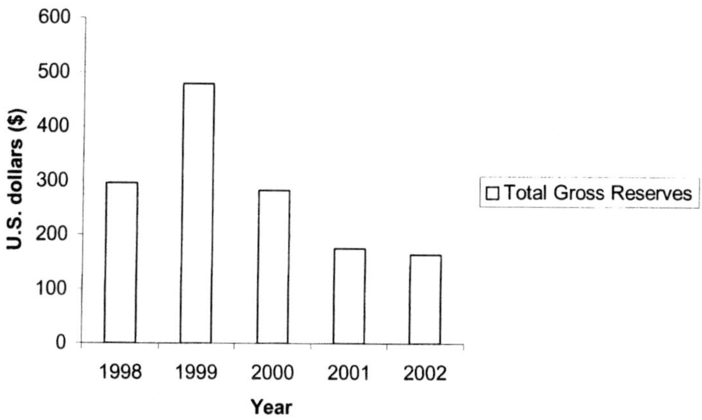

Year	1998	1999	2000	2001	2002
Total Gross Reserves (in millions of US$)	296	479	283	176	165

Source: IMF Report 03/225, July 2003, p. 125. These numbers include pledged and illiquid assets.

Here was a case where one could not blame the drought, mismanaged government parastatals, or the problems from the land reform movement. Gold is a commodity with a globally recognized value, which does not depreciate, or rust from disuse. The mines in Zimbabwe are privately owned, and plenty of gold remains to be mined. It would seem to be the ideal area for Zimbabwe to step up production during a critical period of economic decline. So what happened?

Through 1999 and 2000, as discussed earlier; The Reserve Bank of Zimbabwe (RBZ) was increasingly and desperately short of hard currency. Mugabe's government needed a "currency" that was internationally acceptable, to pay off its ever increasing international loans. Indeed, the IMF banned the government from further borrowing, due to its failure to make timely debt payments.

In late 2001, The Reserve Bank of Zimbabwe (RBZ) came up with what would turn out to be a tremendously ill-conceived solution. It decreed that all gold producers had to sell their gold directly to the RBZ. In return, the RBZ would pay for the gold in Zimbabwean dollars, at the official fixed rate of Z$55 to 1 U.S. dollar.[69] No other commodity markets faced such a binding restriction.

The government claimed in late 2001 that a floor price of Z$23,650 per ounce of gold was a "reasonable platform", given that this translated to $430 per ounce at the official exchange rate of Z$55 per US$1. As the Chamber of Mines put it, "The gold price support scheme, also known as the floor price, is a policy initiative meant to provide meaningful revenues to gold producers who currently face difficult operating conditions as a result of an unfavorable macroeconomic environment."[70] The problem was that this floor price was not realistic, given that the parallel (street) exchange rate was Z$300 per US$1.[71] This meant that with gold selling on the world market at $313 per ounce in late 2002, Zimbabwean miners were rewarded only about $80 per ounce, after exchanging their Z$23,650 at the parallel rate.

In February 2003, the Mugabe's government finally ratcheted the official exchange rate up to 824 Z$ per US$, but the devaluation was not large enough to help the mines. By this time, the parallel rate had reached nearly 2000 Z$ per US$. To make matters worse, payments from the RBZ were often slow in coming, further hurting the mines' cash-flow position. The RBZ had even promised that 50% of the gold mines' production would be paid in US dollars. The managing director of Falcoln Gold mine in Bulawayo, Andrew Beattie, was quoted as saying he had yet to be paid in foreign currency. With electricity costs rising rapidly, and daily cuts in power, Beattie said the mines could only survive a few more months unless something was done.[72]

The currency, still officially pegged at 824 Z$ per US$, continued to devalue on the parallel exchange throughout 2003. By August, the parallel rate was Z$3,500 per US$, making it increasingly difficult for the owners of gold mines to purchase imported production inputs such as fuel and operating equipment. Now

Zimbabwe's once-productive gold mines are threatened to go the way of its maize and tobacco farms because of poor government policies on behalf of the Mugabe government. The Zimbabwean's government apparently did not see the ramifications, even as their gold assets steadily declined, as seen in Figure 5.4.

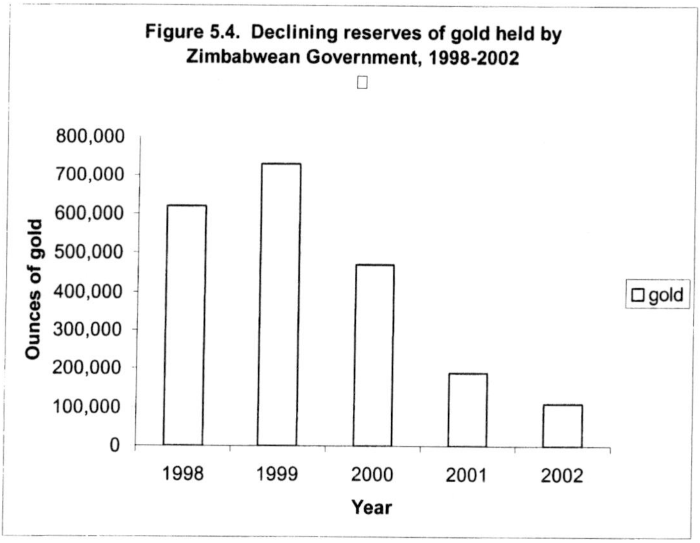

Year	1998	1999	2000	2001	2002
Ounces of gold	620,000	730,000	470,000	190,000	110,000

Some prospects for other mineral resources

As seen in Table 5.1, production levels of nickel, platinum and copper went through tremendous swings in production from 1998 through 2002, as gold production continued to decline. With world prices for these commodities remaining more or less stable (with the exception of soaring platinum prices) the large drop-off in sales of gold was partially offset by increasing production of platinum. While these other commodities remained insulated from the straitjacket government policies that faced gold producers, the plummeting Zimbabwean dollar still meant it was becoming rapidly more expensive for all mineral producers to maintain and invest in new equipment, which was purchased from abroad.

Table 5.1. Zimbabwe Mineral production, prices (US$) and total revenue earned from mineral production. (1998-2002)

	Mineral	unit	1998	1999	2000	2001	2002
Production	nickel	met. tons	10,135	9,594	5,958	8,145	8,092
	platinum	kg	2,730	390	504	519	2,306
	copper	met. tons	2,941	4,977	558	2,056	2,502
	gold	kg	25,175	27,114	22,069	18,050	15,469
	Mineral	unit	1998	1999	2000	2001	2002
World price	nickel	$ per mt	$4,648	$6,030	$8,637	$5,945	$6,772
	platinum	$ per kg	$12,046	$12,186	$17,664	$17,140	$17,447
	copper	$ per mt	$1,609	$1,548	$1,813	$1,578	$1,556
	gold	$ per kg	$9,484	$9,002	$9,002	$8,713	$9,902
Total Revenue (millions of US $)	Mineral		1998	1999	2000	2001	2002
	nickel		$47.1	$57.9	$51.5	$48.4	$54.8
	platinum		$32.9	$4.7	$8.9	$8.9	$40.2
	copper		$4.7	$7.7	$1.0	$3.2	$3.8
	gold		$238.8	$244.1	$198.8	$157.3	$153.2
	Total		$323.5	$314.4	$260.0	$217.8	$252.1

Sources: Countrywatch.com, World Bank Pink Sheets, Zimbabwe Chamber of Mines.

Many of Zimbabwean's mines were partially owned by companies from countries such as Australia, South Africa, Japan, and Ghana. The increasingly rapid devaluation of the Zimbabwean dollar, with no end in sight, told these investors it was time to pull up their holdings, cut their losses, and invest elsewhere in the world. Zimbabwe, by 2002, was losing hundreds of millions of dollars in direct foreign investment in the mining sector, contributing to "capital flight."[73] There was one bright spot that remained, and it remained solely because of the surprisingly "hands-off" attitude of the government.

Platinum- the bright spot for the future?

In August of 2003 a report by analyst Steve Shepherd of JP Morgan Securities revealed some startling facts: Zimbabwe may be sitting on the largest platinum ore deposits in the world.[74] Moreover, the ore deposits are close to the surface, and far less expensive to extract than in South Africa, its primary competitor. Even more attractive to mining companies, Zimbabwe's tax burden is lighter than South Africa's. In light of this, the industry does show bright spots. A private firm, Zimbabwe Platinum Mines (ZIMPLATS), produced more platinum in 2002 than the entire country had produced in 1998. Moreover, a company report revealed that ZIMPLATS had the astonishing potential to produce close to *60,000 kg annually*, roughly a production increase of 2000% for that mine alone, by the year 2006.[75] In addition, the J.P. Morgan report detailed that another large platinum mine, Mimosa, could produce upwards of 5500 kg annually by the year 2025, given sufficient demand and resolving of technical issues. (Mimosa is a joint platinum operation owned by a company in South Africa named IMPLATS and another company in Australia called Aquarius Limited.) The report concluded "assuming political problems in Zimbabwe are resolved over time, we believe it would be logical for IMPLATS to shift from Rustenburg (South Africa) towards Zimbabwe."

So why were the platinum mines increasing production even as the gold mines were closing their doors? For one, the skyrocketing platinum prices were spurring production. But more importantly, Zimbabwe's government took a different tack with platinum, perhaps because they had little to lose, given platinum's small contribution to GDP. They allowed platinum producers to sell directly on the open market, bypassing the government agencies. In addition, the producers were allowed to keep their U.S. dollar earnings in offshore accounts.

Rather than being subjected to the punitive official rate, the industry can exchange dollars at the parallel rate for the Zimbabwean dollar. [76] This has gone a long way towards protecting the mines from the runaway inflation rate, and allowed them to make the profits necessary to keep them in business. Clearly, the prospects of these future profits coaxed them to jointly invest over $200 million dollars in mining operations.[77] Anglo American Platinum (AngloPlat) began development of its Unki platinum mine in July of 2003. IMPLATS and Aquarius also announced plans to invest heavily in Zimbabwe around this time.[78]

Longer term analysis: The potential

According to the IMF Country Report, Zimbabwe's estimated GDP was $7.1 billion (1996 base) dollars in 2002.[79] Using figures from the JP Morgan report, and assuming highly conservative platinum prices of $10,000 per kg (they reached $19,000 per kg in 2001), the operating revenue from ZIMPLATS mine *alone* could pump $600 million dollars into the economy annually by the year 2025. With other platinum mines opened, and gold production resumed to 1998 levels, the economy's platinum output could jump by nearly a billion U.S. dollars, or 14 percent. The story of gold and platinum reveals the dramatic difference in economic performance due to differences in two government policies. As the old phrase goes, "An open hand holds more sand than a closed fist." In any event, the potential remained a distant but achievable goal.

Driving Forces Behind the Rising Deficits

As we have seen, in the three years since 2000, Zimbabwe's severely devalued currency lost more than 99 percent of its value on the parallel market. Given its reliance on imports, Zimbabwe now had new worries. More than ten percent of the economy's income is generated by public enterprises (known as parastatals), which are regulated and subsidized by the government. The top eight (out of thirty) include Air Zimbabwe, the Cold Storage Company, Grain Marketing Board, National Oil Company of Zimbabwe, National Railways of Zimbabwe,

Post and Telecommunications Corporation, Zimbabwe Electricity Supply Authority and Zimbabwe Iron and Steel Company.[80] The enterprises' deficits added up faster than before, as they needed to trade on the parallel market at extremely high rates in order to secure dollars. The enterprises borrowed to make up for their over-spending, through either the commercial banking system or issuing their own bonds, crowding out private investment in the process.[81]

Figure 5.5. Government Spending Outpaces Tax Revenue

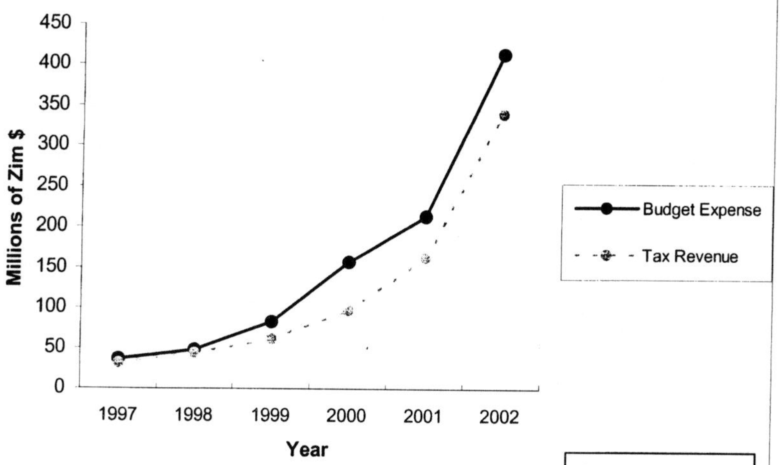

Source: IMF

Although in 2002 the enterprises as a whole technically managed a very slight profit, there were enormous losses in some of the enterprises. The Grain Marketing Board losses alone were equal to 1.5 percent of GDP. The Cold Storage Company, responsible for exporting meat, had losses equal to 570 percent of total revenue from meat sales.[82] Total debt of the major enterprises was Z$115.7 billion by the end of 2002. The enterprises also carried a foreign debt of US$630 million, with the electric, telephone and iron and metal enterprises responsible for 90 percent of this above number. Like the private sector, the public enterprises dealt with foreign exchange shortages with great difficulty, and gradually declined in economic health.[83]

Privatization strategies do exist, and the Zimbabwean government formed the Privatization Agency of Zimbabwe to lead, advise and manage the privatizing of public enterprises into private firms. But the process is going very slowly now, since the isolation of Zimbabwe from international lending agencies like the World Bank.

Figure 5.6. Zimbabwe: Ever-growing National Debt

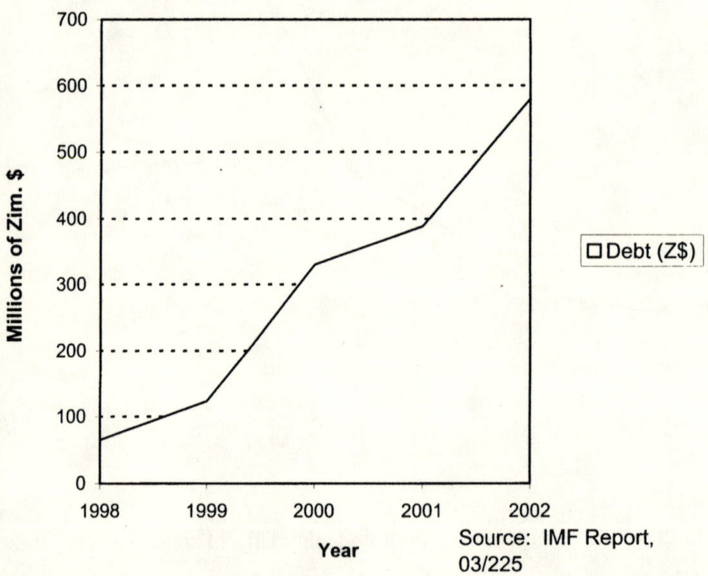

Source: IMF Report, 03/225

The growing cash crunch

In the meantime, the farming sector was in tatters, mining operations were shutting down, and tourism was dropping. Government expenditures were quickly outpacing revenues, as the farm failures rippled through the economy, cutting off tax revenue. The lack of foreign currency was now hurting the communal farmers, causing shortages of seed, fertilizer and fuel, which in turn led to a drop in the production on the communal farms.[84] The government's response in the midst of the cash crunch was to sell increasingly large numbers of Treasury securities to finance the deficits, as tax revenues sharply fell. Borrowing by 2001 reached twenty percent of its budget, as seen below in Figure 5.5. Unfortunately, there were few takers, since the government securities paid interest rates far below the inflation rate. The real rate of return was negative, hardly an attractive investment for private investors.

Under pressure from the Mugabe government, there was one newly willing buyer, however, with almost limitless supplies of cash. That was Zimbabwe's Central Bank. However, that exchange carried with it a devil's bargain, one that would ultimately damage Zimbabwe as badly as its trampled property rights.

Figure 5.7. Sources of Income to Zimbabwean Government, 2001.

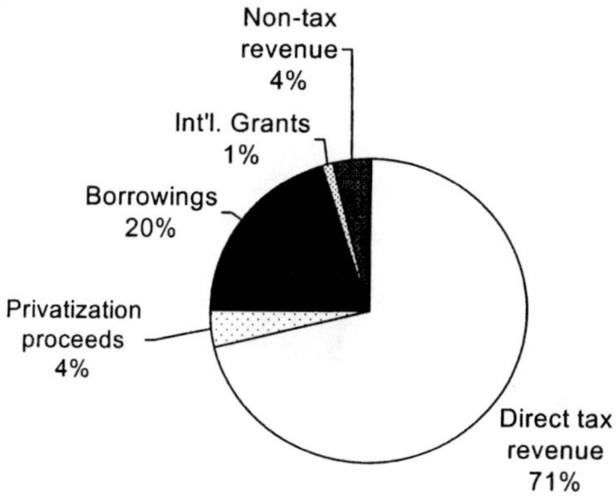

Source: IMF Report 03/225.

Tempting Target: The Reserve Bank of Zimbabwe

Origins and Primary Focus

Like the United States Federal Reserve, Zimbabwe's central bank, (known as the Reserve Bank of Zimbabwe (RBZ)) was originally designed to have a large measure of autonomy from the executive branch, which is critically important in any country in order to help keep inflation in check and unemployment low. When central banks become answerable to failing fiscal policies, politicians often find it easier to print money than raise taxes or cut back on government spending. Inflation, sometimes called the "invisible tax", can be blamed by politicians on greedy businessmen, the weather, or unfair import prices, shifting the blame off the poor fiscal policies.

According to the Constitution of Zimbabwe, "The primary objective of the Reserve Bank of Zimbabwe is to protect the value of the currency in the interest of balanced and sustainable economic growth."[85] Unlike most developing countries, Zimbabwe's central bank started out with a very conservative and unusual position: It chose to use monetary targeting as its strategy for monetary policy, and acknowledged that monetary growth was highly correlated to inflation, as expected. In a correlation test conducted using data from 1980-1999, monetary growth was found to be positively and highly correlated to inflation.[86]

As the banker to the Zimbabwean government, RBZ normally performed various normal banking services such as handling accounts of government departments, and making short term advances to Government. By acting as banker to the Government, the central bank is in a better position to externally judge the general financial condition of Government and give appropriate advice and/or take the necessary remedial action. In addition, the Reserve Bank manages the Government debt, acts as registrar of Government stock and conducts the Treasury bill tenders.

The levers by which the RBZ controls the money supply also mirror the United States system, as seen with the key policies below:

Interest rate policy - In Zimbabwe it is known as the bank rate, similar to the U.S. discount rate. It is the interest rate at which banks borrow from each other and which indirectly influences other interest rates.

Reserve requirements - Known as statutory requirements in Zimbabwe, it is similar to American reserve requirements. This is a stated fraction of all deposits that every bank must keep in the central bank.

Open market operations - This is the process of buying and selling securities or debt in order to either expand or contract the money supply. This is the process mainly used by both the Fed and RBZ in implementing monetary policy, and is normally kept separate from fiscal policy objectives (such as financing deficits).

Thus, RBZ conducts open market operations in a way that is almost identical to the Fed. They buy and sell Treasury bills on behalf of the Zimbabwean government and RBZ bills. They sell both in auctions and through Repurchase agreements (repos). The bank also oversees commercial banks and provides depositors protection against bank failures, by giving them limited protection against bank failures. Thus the RBZ had a strong institutional foundation for protecting the nation's money supply.

The end of autonomy for RBZ

By 2001 the autonomy of the RBZ from the executive branch was crumbling quickly. With deficits running at twenty percent of total government expenditures and few willing buyers of Treasury notes, the RBZ picked up the check by printing millions of Zimbabwean dollars. As a result, the money supply jumped up dramatically, followed quickly by runaway inflation. By the end of 2003, inflation reached more than 500 percent, as seen in the Figures 5.6 and 5.7 below. This, then, was the raw edge of the devil's bargain.

Consider this: Under the "What's New" column at the RBZ's official website, there was in 2003 only one rather eerie article, as seen below in its entirety. It was posted by the RBZ in 2002.

"Bank Acquires New Note Processing Machines"

Zimbabwe is currently experiencing high levels of inflation. The inflationary pressures have emanated from money supply growth rates which are largely inconsistent with economic activity, supply bottlenecks and periodic adjustments to prices of fuel and electricity. These pressures have seen the demand for currency for transaction purposes rising. For example, the number of notes and coins in circulation has risen from $2.2 billion in 1995 to $22.6 billion as of September 2001.

This phenomenal growth in currency in circulation illustrates the need to enhance the distribution and sorting capacities of currency in order to adequately meet demand requirements.

The limitations especially in processing and sorting capacity have created problems such as deterioration in quality of notes in circulation, squeeze on vault space, increased printing costs, increased risk in terms of pilferage, increased cash in transit costs among others.

In an attempt to address these problems arising from stock of unsorted notes, the Bank has acquired high speed note processing machines and a bulk shredder. The note processing machines will facilitate clearance of the current backlog as well as stop accumulation of backlogs arising from daily deposit inflows. On the other hand, the bulk shredder will facilitate easy destruction of the lower denominations as well as soiled notes, in-house without cash movement risks and other related costs.

Source: http://www.rbz.co.zw/new/newnotemachines.htm

What is interesting is that the RBZ indirectly acknowledged the source of the inflation in the second sentence- put more forcefully it could have read "too much money chasing too few goods." The article (and lack of other articles) also makes it clear that the RBZ has gone from a manager of the money supply to mere manufacturer. Unfortunately this manufacturer now has difficulty purchasing inputs such as ink and paper, just like others in the economy.

An economy without well-secured property rights and a secure money supply is the surest recipe for a plunge into unmitigated chaos. The health and education sectors, once the pride of Zimbabwe, were inevitably next to feel the impact.

Figure 5.8. Zimbabwe: Consumer price inflation 1998-2003

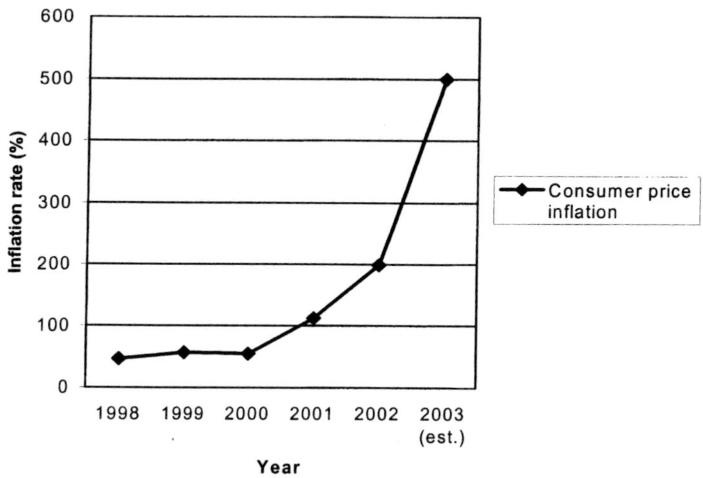

Figure 5.9. Zimbabwe: Money Supply Growth: 1997-2002 (in millions of Z$)

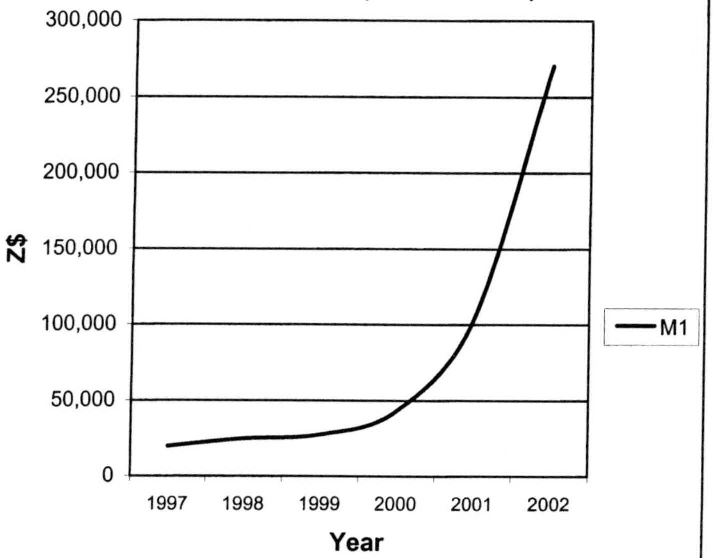

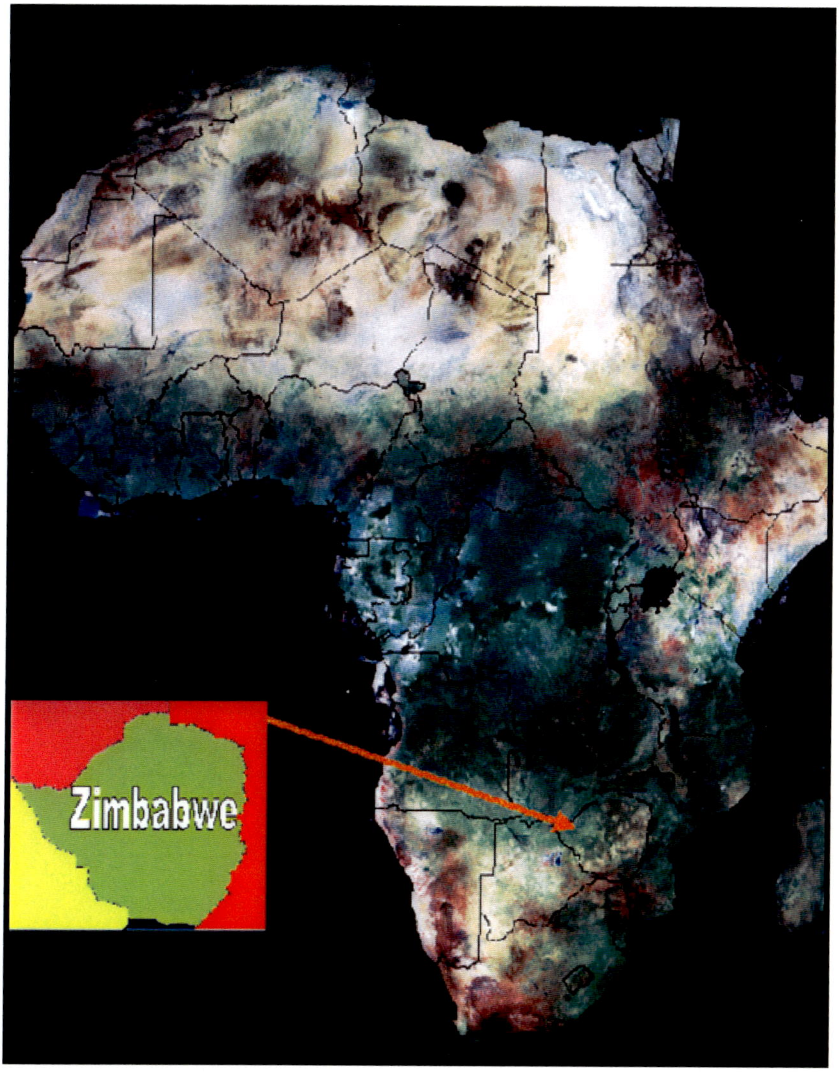

Photo 1. NASA Landsat satellite photo of Africa. Note that Zimbabwe is experiencing severe land degradation in the east even though neighboring areas in Mozambique are green. Green areas indicate high levels of vegetation. This land degradation is the result of communal farming, and there is evidence that this has altered weather patterns, making it increasingly dry and hot in those regions. Used with kind permisssion of Earthsat.com and Stephen Prince of the Geography Department at the University of Maryland. *See also:* http://www.geog.umd.edu/LGRSS/Projects/zimbabwe/ for more photos.

Photo 2. NASA Landsat satellite photo of Zimbabwe, with administrative boundaries. (Note the sideways orientation: Lake Kariba, the long narrow lake, lies along the northern border.) The small light colored squares primarily in the east and south of Zimbabwe indicate substantial land degradation due to communal farming methods. This is true even in the north, where there is much more rainfall. Larger green squares are commercial farmland or parkland. Used with kind permission of Earthsat.com and Stephen Prince, of the Geography department at University of Maryland. *See also:* http://www.geog.umd.edu/LGRSS/Projects/zimbabwe/ for more photos.

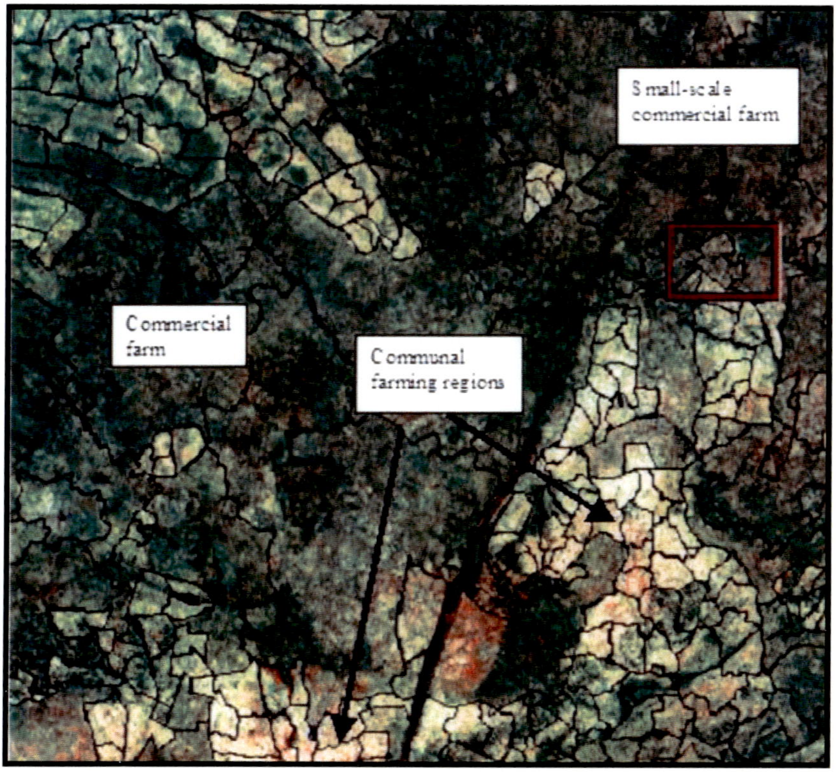

Photo 3. NASA Landsat satellite photo of Zimbabwe, with administrative boundaries in a closer view. Note the small-scale commercial farm has similar coloration to large-scale farms, indicating far better land use than communal farms. The tan areas in the communal lands indicate substantial land degradation. Used with kind permission of Earthsat.com and Stephen Prince, of the Geography department at University of Maryland. *See also:* http://www.geog.umd.edu/LGRSS/Projects/zimbabwe/ for more photos.

Chapter 6. Education, Population and Health Care: From Highs to Lows

Before independence in 1980, white Zimbabweans had far better access to education, health care and land, than did black Zimbabweans. During the 1980s and 1990s, the Mugabe administration had great success in improving blacks' access to education and health care. Unfortunately, the government's approach to land reform in 2000 unintentionally reversed these gains. Although the land reform program was certainly not all to blame, the problems caused by it rippled through the education and health care sectors, and exacerbated the already severe AIDS crisis. This in turn affected the population growth, which is an important determinant in economic growth. This chapter looks at the gains made in the area of health and education, as well as population trends over the past 20 years. It then examines the harmful impact of the land reform movement on these successes.

History of Education

Fifty percent of all blacks were illiterate or semi-illiterate before 1980. In the 1970s, out of every 100 black children, 25 never started school, 33 completed full primary schooling, six went on to secondary school and only three completed secondary schooling.[1] Part of the problem for blacks in the past was the cost of education, and part was access to it. Education cost a significant amount of money, and it cost blacks their children's lost labor time. In addition, even if black families could afford to pay, very few upper primary or secondary schools were within commuting (usually walking) distance, so a boarding school was the only option. To illustrate this, in 1977, over 80% of black employees received under $240 per year, yet $100 was the typical price of boarding schools.[2] Some missionaries did provide nearby education at more reasonable rates, but this was much rarer in rural areas.

The educational system for whites, on the other hand, stood in stark contrast. Despite the fact that their salaries were on average ten times that of blacks, education for all whites was free up to age sixteen (and compulsory). During the 1970s, the government typically spent ten times more on white pupils than black ones. In addition, the teacher/student ratio for whites was twice that for blacks.[3] Not only was this system highly skewed by race, but also by the time the Mugabe government came into power, many schools had been destroyed by war. There was a shortage of qualified teachers, books, and writing materials and other equipment.

Mugabe, a former schoolteacher, now led his country to remarkably rapid gains in education. The new government committed vast resources towards lowering costs and improving access. Primary school was provided free of charge to all citizens. Between 1980 and 1984, 1000 primary schools and 900 secondary schools were built, primarily in rural areas. Thirty thousand teachers (some untrained) were hired in three years, nearly doubling the existing amount. Expenditures on the University of Zimbabwe quadrupled, from Z$8.9 million in 1979/80 to Z$35.3 million in 85/86.[4] By 1990, 96% of all blacks were completing primary school.

Primary enrollment increased from 820,000 in 1979 to 1.2 million in 1980. By 1989 it had leapt to 2.2 million. In the 1990s enrollment peaked at nearly 2.5 million in 1996 before falling to 2.4 million in 2000. At the secondary level the expansion was even more impressive. Enrollment increased from 66,000 in 1979 to 150,000 in 1981, reaching 670,000 in 1989. Secondary enrollment rose to a peak of 844,000 by 2000. Nearly 100% of primary age children were enrolled in school by 2000. College enrollments remained a tiny fraction of the school-age population.[5]

With access to schools vastly improved, Zimbabwe faced the next hurdle: Addressing concerns about the quality of schooling received by many of the students. Here, the greatest concern was the rural areas. Rural areas had teachers, but in most cases they were untrained, and left after a year or two. Poor working conditions, isolation and lack of basic amenities make it difficult to attract anyone, and especially the highly sought trained teachers. Urban centers, on the other hand, had fewer problems in attracting trained staff, and turnover was significantly lower. Not surprisingly, the students' level of learning was at a much superior level. Access was improved by abolishing primary school fees, even though parents still had to pay for transport to school, and the loss of the children's labor.

Not only were there differences between blacks and whites, but there were also differences in access to education by gender. In 1980, 77 girls attended primary school for every 100 boys, but steady progress over the years has meant that by 1999 the ratio was 88 girls to 100 boys.

Costs of education

All of these successes have not come cheaply, however. By 1989, educational expenditures were consuming almost one quarter of the government budget. Zimbabwe ranked fourth out of the 114 listed countries, in terms of percent of GDP devoted to education. The rate of growth had been so high that government officials were becoming concerned about the supply of over-qualified and underemployed individuals coming out into the workforce. By the 1991-92 school year, "free" education was over, and school fees were reintroduced, with uniform fees typically costing $160, which was out of range for some Zimbabweans, although a UNESCO education report said there had been little overall effect on enrollment.[6] Increased funding pressures led to the government requiring that the parents assist in the building of new classrooms, or in some cases, charging levies.[7] Despite the rapid building of schools, there was still a shortage. In addressing the problem, the government instituted the idea of "hot-seating," a system of double sessions, where two groups of students used the same facilities each day. The quality of the teaching was not keeping up either; in 1991 only 30 to 45 percent of the teachers were trained, and there was a "chronic shortage" of textbooks and furniture.[8]

Although a top priority for the Mugabe government, educating the black majority was admittedly expensive. By 2000, it consumed the largest share of the national budget (22%), and 96 percent of its expenses went toward paying teachers, leaving only 4 percent for development.[9] The impact of AIDS also hit the education sector very hard, as will be discussed later in the chapter.

The problem of underemployed graduates

While there were certainly large numbers of students being turned out by the new educational system, by the mid-1990s it was clear that there were more students than jobs, which had led to chronic underemployment of thousands of workers in the economy. The government took action and since 1998, twenty-five vocational centers were built, with programs that are "demand-driven." This means that the local communities are consulted regarding what jobs are needed, and the curriculum is designed to address those local job market needs.

In addition, very few students in the early 1990s had access to a university education, because there was only one university. By the late 1990s, Zimbabwe had vastly increased access to higher education. The number of full-fledged universities increased from one to eight, and three colleges were added as well. Enrollment increased from 9,000 students nationwide to 33,000, an increase of almost 300%. Although there were no new public technical colleges added, the enrollment for these institutions jumped from 1989 to 1999 by 114 percent. Enrollment along gender lines was not balanced, except for teacher colleges, as seen by the Table 6.1. Females were particularly underrepresented in technical colleges, but made their best showing in teachers' colleges.

Table 6.1. A Comparison of Males vs. Females in Zimbabwe's Tertiary Educational Institutions, 2000.

Institutions	Males	Females	Total	% Females
Technical Colleges	10,997	4,501	15,498	29.0
Teachers' Colleges	8,118	9,646	17,764	54.3
Universities	22,526	10,833	33,359	32.5
Total	41,641	24,980	66,621	37.5

Source: UNESCO report, p. 29.

The collapse of the educational system: 2000-2003

The deepening economic and political crisis in Zimbabwe "engulfed the education system from top to bottom," according to a June 2003 article by the London-based Guardian newspaper. Selections from the article provide a vivid portrayal of how the education system has fared since 2000:

The University of Zimbabwe, once the prestigious pinnacle of the system bequeathed by colonial rule, is now finding it almost impossible to keep functioning. Meanwhile, in schools across the country teachers are operating hand to mouth, worrying less about lesson plans than what their pupils have to eat.

At the university, in Harare's Mount Pleasant suburb, clouds of tear gas frequently smother the campus, classrooms and dormitories. In the past few years, police have sealed off the campus so many times that it is almost routine. Once last year riot police stormed into dormitories, dragged students from their rooms and beat them. One student died from his injuries and has become a cause célèbre .

The pay of lecturers and professors is so low that almost all have had to find other jobs and consultancies to get by. So many university posts remain vacant after resignations that departments are decimated and knowledgeable academics say the university is at the point of collapse.

Classes have been suspended and students sent home several times in the past three years, making it difficult for students to finish their degrees in a reasonable period of time.

"I used to enjoy teaching at the university, but now the conditions have become untenable," said a retiring professor. "Now it is a constant headache. There is political interference from political appointees, corruption, the continual battles of police on campus. Far from being an ivory tower removed from everything, the university has become an encapsulation of Zimbabwe's problems."

Other tertiary institutions across the country have faced similar troubles, while in schools teachers have been beaten, forced to attend "re-education camps" and killed, according to union officials. Students of all ages are sent home if they cannot pay fees or don't have proper uniforms. Education budgets have been dropping for more than 10 years. Teachers' meagre salaries have lagged far behind the country's 269% inflation.

The Progressive Teachers' Union of Zimbabwe has documented the intimidation, harassment, detention, arrests, torture and the unprecedented unleashing of state security agents on the schools. As a result of the assaults by state agencies, the union reported that between the period 2000-2002 five teachers were killed, 119 raped and "many more were maimed, kidnapped, tortured and displaced". In addition, many teachers and students have been forced to attend "re-education camps" where lessons centre on a narrow party-oriented history of Zimbabwe, including the formation of the ruling party, Zanu-PF, its military struggle against white- minority Rhodesia and why the party deserves to remain in power. [10]

After 2000, about 15% of Zimbabwean children remained out of school, and a disproportionately high number of those were girls. The country's spiraling economic crisis in the past three years has caused many more children to stop going to school because their parents cannot afford the steeply rising fees and the cost of uniforms and books.

"This problem of dropouts is directly related to the general problem of poverty," said Prof. Raftopoulos, who is an associate professor at the Institute for Development Studies at the University of Zimbabwe. "In a poverty assessment study survey carried out by the United Nations Development Programme, it was found that 61% of Zimbabweans were classified as poor in 1997, rising to 73% in 2003. With more specific references to dropouts, a study of social policy under structural adjustment conditions in Zimbabwe carried out in 1997/98 found that the major reason for children dropping out of school was unaffordability."[11]

While in the mid-1980s Zimbabwe's budget allocation to the sector was more than twice the median of that spent by other low-income Anglophone countries and exceeded the median for medium income countries by about 22%, the toll of the economic crisis has hurt the crowning achievement of Zimbabwe. Real per capita expenditure on education has fallen significantly, with the total education budget allocation declining from 6% of GDP in 1986-87 to 4% in 1993-94. By 2000 real expenditure on primary education had dropped to 2% of GDP.[12]

As real expenditures declined, education fees rose to make up the shortfall. According to a UNICEF report, almost 40% of children of primary school age who dropped out of school reported rising fees as the main reason for quitting. Many children, especially girls, are dropping out of school to care for parents afflicted by HIV or to look after their siblings when their parents die. The report says poverty and HIV/AIDS caused completion rates in primary education to fall to 70 per cent in 1999.[13]

From 2000-2003, Zimbabwe's land seizures hit the education of young children particularly hard. As was discussed earlier, more than 320,000 of Zimbabwe's 350,000 commercial farm workers lost their jobs since 2000. As a result, these unemployed workers cannot afford to send their children to school, and more than 120,000 children in primary and secondary school no longer have access to basic education.[14]

Population Trends

From 1901 to 1982, Zimbabwe's population increased more than tenfold. The population mushroomed because of Zimbabwe's long history of relatively low mortality rates and high fertility rates.[15] From 1969 to 1982 alone, the population grew 47%, and added 2.4 million people. As a result, a large proportion of the population is now under fifteen years old.

Immigration also played a small role in population growth. Immigration statistics were not generally collected, but data from censuses can be used to get some idea of general trends. The number of non-citizens from 1969 to 1982 increased from 272,000 to 528,000, which indicates a fairly large number of immigrants entered the country, most of who were black.

During the late 60s and 70s while many blacks were arriving, whites were exiting, reflecting in many cases the whites' fear of the regime's growing political instability. Many believed that if the black majority gained power, reprisal and land redistribution would follow. An average of 10,000-12,000 whites left the country each year during the seventies.[16] By 1982, the number of whites had plunged to an estimated 148,000 from 230,000 in 1969.[17] Once comprising 6% of the total population in 1961, the white share of the population had fallen to 2% by 1986.[18]

Calculating estimates of these growth rates has been difficult. There have only been three official counts of the black population- in 1962, 1969 and most recently in 1982. Nonetheless, estimates of the total population size and growth of both groups have been calculated since 1901, when the first white-only census was taken. Estimates of the number of blacks originally came from using information on their tax returns, but in 1948 and periodically thereafter, the government conducted a sample survey of villages. The size of the black population was then extrapolated from these surveys. Table 6.2 reports the findings below.

Table 6.2. Population Size By Ethnic Group, 1901 to 1982.

Year	Total	African	European	Asian	Colored	% African in total
1901	711,100	700,000	11,100	N/A	N/A	98.2
1911	906,600	880,000	23,700	900	2,000	97.1
1921	1,147,100	1,110,000	33,800	1,300	2,000	96.8
1931	1,464,200	1,410,000	50,100	1,700	2,400	96.3
1941	2,005,900	1,930,000	69,300	2,600	4,000	96.2
1951	2,828,400	2,680,000	138,000	4,400	6,000	94.8
1961	3,968,000	3,730,000	221,000	7,100	10,400	94.0
1962	4,098,300	3,860,000	220,000	7,400	10,900	94.2
1969	5,134,300	4,880,000	230,000	9,000	15,300	95.1
1982	7,477,443	7,297,242	147,741	10,802	21,648	97.5

Source: 1982 Census of Zimbabwe.

Using these population estimates, growth rates for blacks, whites, and other groups were routinely estimated by Zimbabwe's Census Bureau. The rates climbed steadily up to the year 1961, peaking at 3.5%. After this point, they began declining; from 1962-69 the growth rate was 3.3% and from 1969-82 it dropped further to 3.0%. From 1969-1982 Africans had the highest overall growth rate, at

3.14%, followed by persons in the "Coloured" category at 2.71%, Asians at 1.42% and Europeans at –3.35%. In the 1990s, The World Bank and The United Nations saw high population growth rates as one of the key impediments to economic success, and focused much research and money on trying to slow the growth rates down, in order to increase per-capita GDP.

The Population Growth rate: Then and Now

Zimbabwe's population growth indeed slowed down because of declining fertility, according to a 2000 report by the United Nations Population Fund (UNFPA). The UNFPA said fertility has been declining due to widespread adoption of modern contraception and changing fertility preferences in Zimbabwe. Fertility fell from more than six children per woman in the 1980s to 4.4 in 1994 and about 3.8 in 2003. The report states, "Despite the fall in the growth rate, the size of the population continues to grow as a result of population momentum."[19] What was not predicted, though, was the devastating effect that the HIV/AIDS virus would have in swinging the growth pendulum the other direction. With a rapidly deteriorating economic situation, the population is growing slower, and growing sicker even more quickly. Children now care for their sick parents and siblings, and then are left on their own when their parents die. These orphaned children often turn to vandalism, drop out of school or are exploited as cheap labor. The health care system, considered at one time to be one of the best in Africa, has not been able to keep up with ravages of the virus in the face of a rapidly deteriorating economic situation, as will be discussed in the detail in the next section.

Health Infrastructure and AIDS

Prior to 1980, Zimbabwe's health care sector was split into five sub-sectors that operated more or less independently of each other. They included the Ministry of Health, local authorities, religious missions, industry-based clinics, and private national clinics, along with other voluntary organizations. The private sub-sector provided high quality care mostly for the white community, and the care was generally paid for through private insurance. Some public care was provided through the remaining sub-sectors, but medical facilities were limited or nonexistent in the largely black rural areas. As a consequence, there were nutritional deficiencies in children, communicable diseases, and maternity-related problems.[20] Access to medical care actually worsened during the 1970s; ultimately half of the 360 clinics were damaged or destroyed by war.[21]

After 1980, the Mugabe government sought to transform this imbalance, by having government play a larger role in the provision of health care, particularly in isolated rural communities. Basic medical care for all citizens was the ultimate goal. Immediate steps were taken. Damaged clinics were rebuilt, and some 290 new clinics were constructed. The government put greater emphasis on preventive measures such as education in hygiene and nutrition, immunization programs, and prenatal care and childcare. Activities such as family planning, immunization, nutrition education, and sanitation were now strongly endorsed.[22] The number of doctors and nurses nearly doubled from 1979 to 1984, to nearly 500 and 7,600 respectively, although a shortage of qualified doctors and nurses remains.[23] Many of these doctors arrived from other war-torn or politically unstable African regimes; Ghana in particular lost much of its skilled workforce during the early 80s.

A result of this expansion was an enormous growth in health care expenditures. From 1981 to 1987 health care expenditures spiraled upward, increasing by 11% per year.[24] In 1979 spending was Z$60 million, while in 1987/88 it was Z$286 million.[25] Spending on preventive services alone grew from $4.5 million in 1979/80 to $25.7 million in 1985/86.

The investment appeared to be paying off, at least in health terms. Infant malnutrition fell from 29% in 1980 to 16% in 1984. The percentage of fully immunized children increased from 25% in 1980 to 67% in 1987.[26] Life expectancy rose from 51 in 1970 to 63 in 1988.[27] Infant mortality rates fell from 74 per thousand infants in 1980 to 49 per thousand infants in 1988.[28]

A four-tiered system of service delivery was gradually organized:[29]

First Level:	56	rural hospitals
	927	health centers of which:
	132	are run by the Ministry of Health
	510	are run by local government
	70	are religious based missions
	55	are urban facilities
	160	are industry-owned
Second Level:	55	district hospitals
Third Level:	8	provincial and 4 General Hospitals
Fourth Level:	5	central Hospitals located in Harare and Bulawayo

How did Zimbabwe's health care expenditures then compare to other countries? Zimbabwe's health expenditure as a percent of GNP was 2.3% in 1986, according to United Nations data, as seen in Table 6.3. The UN source labels Zimbabwe a country with "medium human development." Compared to other countries with "medium human development," this was well above the average of 1.5%. Meanwhile, the average for poor countries, those called "low human development," was 0.8%, while for the countries with "high human development," the average was 4.6%.

The sudden drop in life expectancy and the scourge of AIDS

With all the gains made in the 1980s and mid-1990s, Zimbabwe's health system was a model for other developing countries. Unfortunately, the years hence have shattered all the gains, and Zimbabwe has descended to its lowest level in its history. Life expectancy has been slashed by 22 years; half the babies born today will not make it past their 35th birthday. At current trends, if nothing is done, by 2010 newborns will have a life expectancy of only 31 years. Contrast that with life a decade earlier, in 1993, where newborn children were expected to live to 56 years.[30]

Table 6.3. Health expenditures as a percentage of GDP, 1960 vs. 1986.

	1960	1986
All Developing Countries	0.9	1.4
Least developed Countries	0.7	0.9
Sub Saharan Africa	0.7	0.8
Industrial Countries	2.2	4.7
World	2.0	4.2
Zimbabwe	1.2	2.3

Source for table and figure: World Bank.

Figure 6.1. Zimbabwe: Plunging Life Expectancy

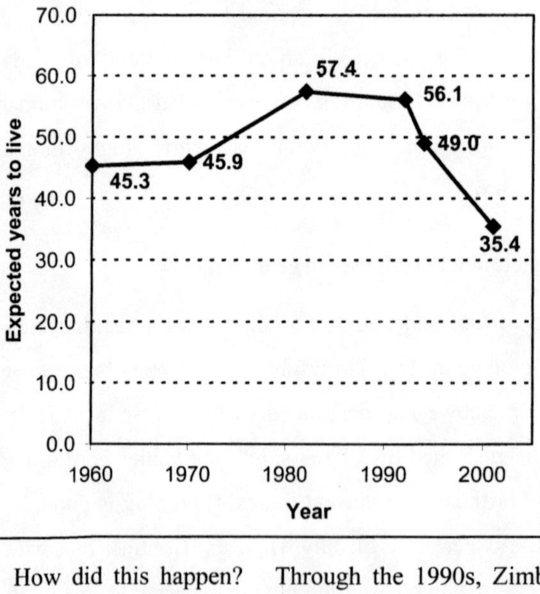

How did this happen? Through the 1990s, Zimbabwe's health and health service indicators hit a wall or began reversing direction, brought on primarily by epidemic of AIDS. It is nearly impossible to overstate the impact of AIDS.

UNAIDS estimated that by the end of 2001 more than 750,000 children were orphaned, a greater percentage than anywhere else in the world. Every week in 2002, another 2,500 people died of the disease.[31] By the end of this decade, over one million people in Zimbabwe are projected to lose their lives to AIDS.[32] The skyrocketing costs of treating the illness are exacerbated because hospital billing procedures are outmoded and inefficient, resulting in a loss of millions of dollars because the government is not collecting insurance claims.[33]

Unfortunately, the government offered scant leadership for educating Zimbabweans for quite some time (although now AIDS education is part of the curriculum), and offered punitive responses instead. For example, beginning in 1996, AIDS patients who suffered kidney ailments were barred from receiving dialysis treatment, which sped up their deaths. This was the first time patients with incurable illnesses were turned away from government-provided health services.[34] In July of 1997, legislation was introduced that enabled courts to punish deliberate HIV transmitters.[35] It was not until 2003 that the government even allocated any money towards the purchase of anti-retroviral drugs useful in fighting AIDS, despite over Z$7 billion allocated towards health care.[36]

Because of AIDS, the demand and supply of education are likely to drop over the medium term, as pointed out by the IMF. School enrollments have declined, as children have returned home to care for sick or dying parents. Large numbers of teachers and administrators have died, and another study cited by the IMF predicts that 83 percent of the total 2003 teacher workforce will be dead by 2010, and says that "this scenario paints a grim picture for medium to long-term growth in Zimbabwe."[37] More importantly, it underscores the tremendous duress yet to borne by the already suffering Zimbabwean people.

A number of international agencies, including the World Health Organization, CDC, USAID, and UNAIDS, are helping to fight this battle through a number of different actions, including the push for further education, distribution of condoms, training of health-care professionals, as well as voluntary support activities for orphaned children.

Figure 6.2. HIV Seroprevalence for Zimbabwean Pregnant Women, 1990-97

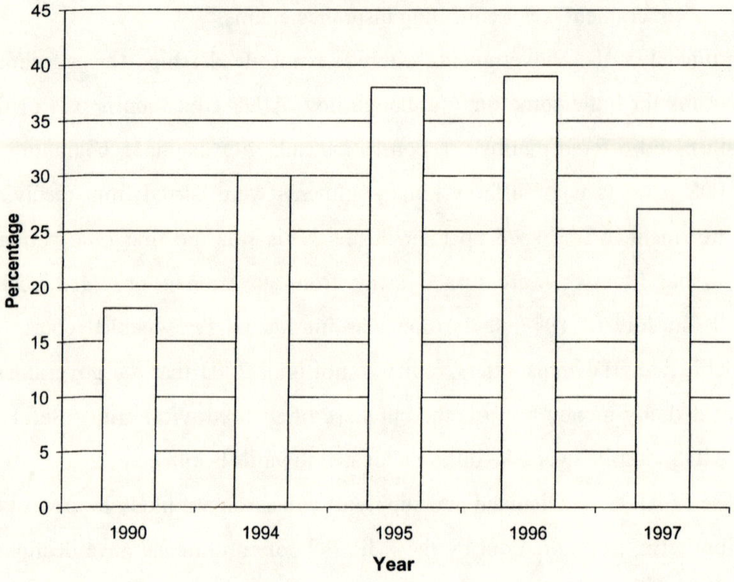

All of this activity must be met by changes in behavior on the part of Zimbabweans or it will prove extremely difficult to stop the onslaught of this disease. Otherwise, a vicious cycle of poverty may develop where Zimbabwe continues to spiral downward, because of productivity and human capital losses related to HIV/AIDS.

A relationship between land seizures and AIDS deaths?

It is no doubt a large stretch, at first blush, to link the rising AIDS cases with land seizures and general economic conditions. AIDS cases were on the rise before the land seizures, and reflected poor government leadership, as well as local taboos against using birth control. Yet one can make the argument that an economy spiraling ever downward could make a bad problem worse.

Taking charge of AIDS cases in relative economic calm might be feasible, but in the midst of a chaotic economic storm it has proved nearly impossible. Hyperinflation, shortages of food and hard currency affect doctors and nurses as much as other Zimbabweans. Many of these health professionals are fleeing the country, leaving the health care system crumbling even more quickly. It is not surprising that when a country is facing starvation, the AIDS crisis must necessarily take a lower priority. In addition, the economic storm now faced by Zimbabwe may possibly change some people's perceptions about risky sexual behavior.

Modeling risky behavior

Controversially, researchers have modeled risky sexual behavior, and noted that standard cost-benefit analysis can be applied to how people acquire AIDS.[38] When the marginal cost of acquiring AIDS drops, these models predict that more individuals will engage in risky sexual behaviors, such as having sex without a condom. Here, the marginal cost to the individual is defined as everything the individual would lose out on in life after acquiring AIDS, both financially and psychologically. Note that individuals do make many choices today about things that will affect them after they are gone, such as the purchase of life insurance.

Unfortunately, this hypothesis seems to be bearing out in the United States. In the late 1990s, so-called AIDS cocktail drugs became available. These drugs not only prolonged people's lives, they also increased the quality of life to nearly the same as before the onset of the disease. As a result, the marginal cost of risky behavior dropped. As the theory predicts, young people in the ages 13-24 in the United States are now once again engaging in higher risk behaviors, such as using condoms less frequently, and having more partners, according to the Center for Disease Control.[39]

In Zimbabwe, AIDS drugs are far less available (indeed, cheap generic imports were only available in 2002), but the marginal cost of risky behavior has dropped in an even more significant way, making risky sex less foreboding, through a cruel set of circumstances. First, if life grows more miserable, then people may feel there is less missed out on by the possibility of exiting early. For example, if people have seen their friends, children, their spouses, and their parents die at an early age, many will feel there is less to live for. Second, with unemployment reaching 70 percent in some regions, there are few economic opportunities left either. As a result, the economic model predicts people will take fewer precautions, having far less to lose.

There is some data to tentatively support this hypothesis. Despite educating Zimbabwean men, many have still not changed their sexual behavior. By 1998 most adult Zimbabweans understood that in order to prevent AIDS, condoms and having only one sexual partner were important, as seen in Figure 6.3. Yet more than 1 in 3 infected men, who are the primary transmitters, admitted that they still did not change their dangerous behavior once they had contracted AIDS, nor did they bother to inform their partner. In addition, an astonishing 79% of females said that upon learning that they had a sexually transmitted disease, they did nothing to avoid infecting their partner.[40]

It is important to note that these responses do not allow one to conclude that land seizures caused people to engage in risky behavior. That would be too simplistic a conclusion. As was stated earlier, AIDS was an ongoing problem well before that time, and the disease also afflicts other countries that have not faced land reforms. However, it is worth contemplating that the collapse of Zimbabwe may have exacerbated to some degree an already terrible problem.

Figure 6.3. Knowledge of Ways to Prevent HIV/AIDS, 1998.

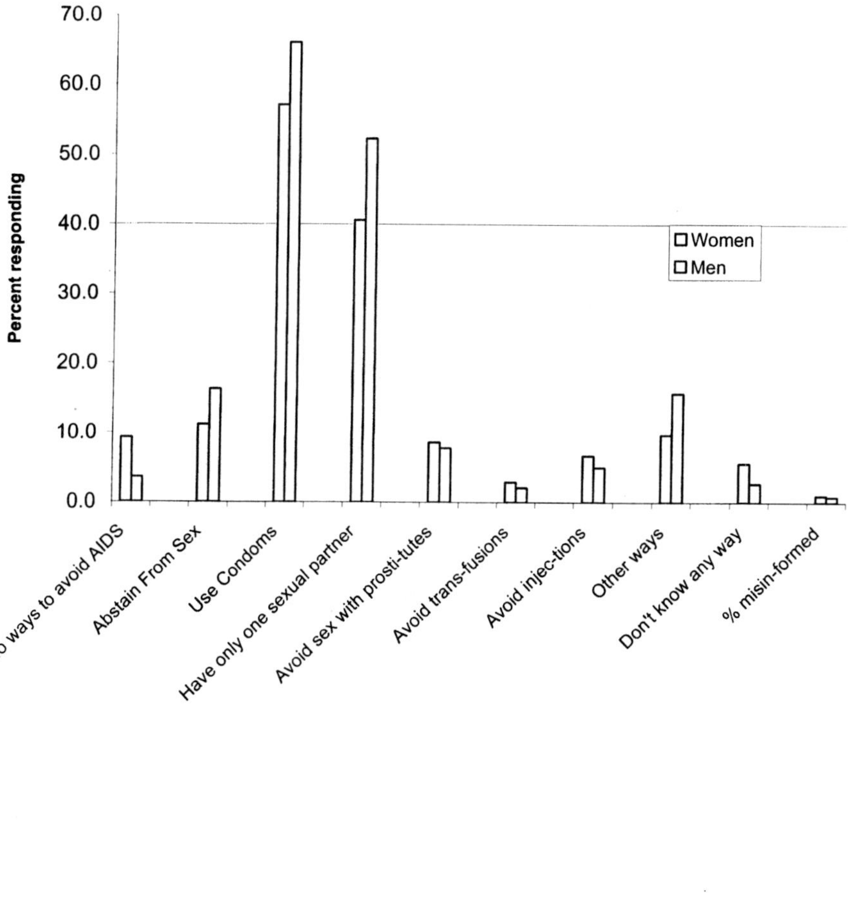

Chapter 7. The Labor Market and Women's Role in it

The Structure of the Labor Force

Another way to understand the longstanding appeal for land reform, from the black Zimbabweans' perspective, is by examining the friction caused by the long-term differences in wages between blacks and whites. This chapter argues that after a number of years of slowly improving working conditions for blacks, real wages began to slip in the late 1990s, putting more pressure on the government to do something. Unfortunately, turning to fast-track land reform as an antidote quickly undid most of the progress that had been made. In addition, the negative consequences of the land reform hit women disproportionately harder than men. Of those Zimbabweans who benefited from land reform, women benefited the least, and usually not at all.

The labor market before 1980

The Ministry of Finance, in the 1965-1979 period, reported wage data in two classifications: 1) Africans and 2) Europeans, Asians and Coloreds. Africans generally earned one-tenth of what Europeans and others earned, largely because of racially based job classifications that prevented them from seeking higher paying jobs. After 1979, the Mugabe-led Ministry of Finance did not publish wage data breakdowns by race, for unknown reasons.

However, one may discern the relative welfare of the Africans (blacks) by examining the trends in wages in occupations dominated by them. In general, nominal wages in occupations dominated by blacks rose steeply during the first decade of the Mugabe regime. For example, agricultural workers, who make among the lowest wages, saw the largest gains in the early 1980s, with average monthly wages climbing 150% from 1980-1983.[1] In occupations with the highest wage levels, such as finance, wages grew at a more moderate 43% during this period. Income gaps between blacks and whites narrowed somewhat. But were the gains real, after adjusting for inflation? The numbers indicate a mixed story. From 1980 to 1983 prices increased approximately 75 percent. Agriculture, private domestic and mining sectors posted real increases in wages over this time, while employees in all other sectors lost purchasing power. Unfortunately, aggregate statistics are not available on wage rates after 1984. The Central Statistical Office stopped collecting wage information on agricultural workers, so wage information is available only on a sector basis, excluding agriculture.

The labor market during the Mugabe years

Prior to independence in 1980, Zimbabwe had minimum wages in various sectors, but after independence a national policy was enacted, which applied minimum wages on a much larger scale, in an attempt to rectify past inequities. In addition, racially based job classifications were abolished during this time.[2] Minimum wages were raised across all the sectors, with some sectors much more than others. For example, mining workers received around twice the wage hike of agricultural workers.[3]

On the other hand, higher minimum wages "tend to exacerbate the decline, or slow growth in employment levels, as industry tends to use more labor-saving techniques," the Ministry of Finance stated in its 1985 *Socioeconomic Review*.[4] This increase in wages had large impacts in the agricultural sector, which increased mechanization and labor saving techniques in response to a rise in wage rates. Average annual employment levels declined an average of 4% per year from 1980 to 1984.[5]

Also affected was the mining sector, which employs large numbers of unskilled workers; employment levels also fell by 4% per year from 1980-1984. Other sectors were either less affected or not at all, because the minimum-wage floor remained below equilibrium wages.[6]

As unemployment rose, this partially caused wage stagnation, since there was a large pool of unemployed workers to draw upon. The minimum wage policies, while intended to help blacks, had made things worse for the growing number of workers without jobs. In addition, large government deficits led to price supports being lifted in 1998. As basic food staples and fuel shot up in price, riots erupted throughout the country. Security forces intervened where necessary to keep the populace under control.[7] By 2001 the government could no longer avoid raising prices again, and the price of food almost doubled between January and August. For example, bread in August cost 50 Z$, up from 23 Z$ in January. Fuel prices were hiked up by 74 percent, and bus fares went up 50 percent.

In an attempt to divert attention from the government's missteps, Mugabe launched more speeches, declaring white commercial farmers "enemies of the state."[8] Mugabe encouraged ZANU-PF supporters to take over more white commercial farms. With 60 percent of the country's non-farm enterprises directly or indirectly dependent on commercial agriculture activity, many manufacturing firms closed or announced major retrenchments, as farm seizures continued. The unintended consequences for black Zimbabweans are that the formal-sector unemployment now exceeds 70 percent, and hundreds of thousands of black farm and manufacturing workers have lost their jobs. Sectors not linked to farming have also suffered. For example, tourist traffic dropped sharply under the perception of political chaos and lawlessness, leading to layoffs in these sectors as well. As shown in Chapter 5, the mining sector was also deeply affected. The collapse of the farming sector thus rippled across the economy, collapsing other sectors like falling dominos.

Triple-digit inflation in 2002 further exacerbated worker tensions; strikes and protests by workers disrupted various activities including mineral production and transportation. The call for land distribution in the name of redistributive equity had sharply backfired, and most Zimbabweans were worse off than before as a result. Not only was there more unemployment, but also the nature of the work itself was changing. The labor force can be divided into two sectors: the informal sector and the formal sector. By understanding the nature of these sectors, we can get a better understanding of which groups were most affected by the land seizures, and how the nature of this work changed after the land reforms.

The formal versus informal sector

Workers who operate in the informal sector do not generate any revenue for the government and are not registered or licensed. Operators of fruit stands, market stalls, and underground activities fall into this sector. Individuals typically work much longer hours for much less pay than in the formal sector.[9] It is not reported in quarterly economic data, in contrast to the formal sector, so depending on assumptions, those workers are sometimes considered unemployed.

Through the sixties and early seventies, the formal labor force grew steadily, yet between 1975 and 1985 it hovered around 1,000,000 workers despite a rapidly growing population. The informal sector and/or unemployment have grown because of the difficulties the economy had in absorbing the burgeoning labor force. As we have seen, many educated people found few jobs waiting for them after their schooling was completed. Women also played an increasing role in the labor force, because of a higher proportion achieving an education than in years past. As the *Zimbabwe Statistical Yearbook 1987* points out, Zimbabwe has long had problems with creating new jobs in the formal sector at a rate that satisfies the population growth.[10] Along with its minimum wage policies, this structural imbalance in the labor market led to a decade of wage stagnation. These conditions made Zimbabwe particularly vulnerable to the conditions leading to economic collapse.

When comparing labor force statistics for men and women from 1982, one also notes striking differences in their labor force participation rates, as evidenced by Table 7.1. Women held only 15% of all jobs in the formal economy and were about five times more likely than men to work in the informal sector.

Occupational classifications

Men and women show very different occupational patterns. The formal sector is divided into eight categories by the Census Bureau, but two make up the bulk of the workers: 1) Agriculture, Animal Husbandry and Forestry at 61.2%, and Production and Related Workers at 15.6%. When these distributions are broken down by gender, the distinctions become even more dramatic. Seventy-six percent of all women in the labor force work in the agriculture sector, compared with 51% of all men. Men dominate the production category, having six times as many of those jobs as women. Twenty-two percent of all men's jobs were in production, contrasting with a scant 5.5% of all women's jobs.[11] Thus the post 2000 economic crisis affected men and women differently, with women bearing the brunt of the crisis in the early stages, since agriculture was the first sector to be affected.

Table 7.1. Labor market classifications, by sex

	Men	Women	Women's Percent of total
Formal sector	47%	8%	14.5%
Informal sector	1%	5%	83.3%
Unemployed	9%	5%	35.7%
Farming	24%	29%	54.7%
Economically Inactive	20%	53%	72.6%
Total	100%	100%	

Source: *Zimbabwe Statistical Yearbook*, 1987.

The Predicament of Women in Zimbabwe

Women as family providers

Under severe economic consequences such as the current economic crisis, women in Zimbabwe bear the brunt of it, since they are primarily responsible for running the household.[12] With official unemployment rates over fifty percent, women fulfill a primary role, by earning income for their families in the informal sector. This often involves petty trading, selling handicrafts, buying and selling fruits and vegetables, brewing beer, raising small livestock, and so on.[13] Even in normal times, men are not typically seen as the primary breadwinners. For example, in a survey of 79 women in 1993, none of the husbands were contributing even half of the estimated amount of income needed to feed a family of six, as estimated by the Zimbabwean Central Statistical Office.[14]

In addition to earning income, the typical Zimbabwean women are busy with household tasks and chores throughout the day. They include cooking and cleaning, and possibly gardening, looking after pre-school children, and caring for the elderly, disabled and chronically ill.[15] With the increase in AIDS, their burden in the latter area has multiplied many-fold, exhausting them and preventing many women from attending school.

In agricultural areas, the women perform all food-related activities, including caring for seed, plowing, planting, weeding, harvesting, and preparing the meals. Occasionally men will be in charge of the plowing, especially if tractors are available. One study showed women in sub-Saharan Africa do about 70% of all the agricultural work.[16]

The burdened lives of women may stem from the European conquest of Africa. Before this time, felling trees, hunting and warfare were the chief preoccupations of the African men. Felling and hunting became less important as Zimbabweans were forced into designated areas, often with poor vegetation. In some cases the Europeans prevented the Africans from fighting each other. In any event the men often saw little to do, as their traditional roles disappeared. They often resisted helping their wives in "women's work." In some cases the men emigrated from the region in search of market wages, or were recruited by Europeans to work in mines, road building or other heavy work.[17]

Yet despite women being the country's workhorses, their status and rights remain far below that of men, like much of sub-Saharan Africa. Under the law, married women become the property of men (although ironically those same men may now not own a farm). Examining this difference in social status will help us understand the differential impact of the land reforms on men versus women.

The social status of women

The historic custom of a brideprice, still prevalent in traditional African communities today, strongly characterizes women's status in Zimbabwe. A brideprice is a market transaction between the bride-giving and the bride-receiving family, involving the transfer of livestock, or more recently money, in exchange for a bride. This exchange establishes the marriage between the spouses and is essentially a business proposition between the elders of the two families. The bride is sold to the groom's family as a labor resource. In addition, the husband and his family obtain future labor resources from any children she might bear.[18] The husband expects total submission from his wife, for life.

If a family paid for their daughter to go to school, then they expect recompense as part of the brideprice.[19] Women have traditionally not been encouraged to get an education, probably at least in part because it was difficult for the bride's family to recover the full amount through the brideprice.

The social status of a woman is almost completely determined by her success in bearing children through marriage. Once married, the woman drops her last name and is addressed by that of her spouse, as the wife of "X". This indicates a new and more prestigious status. If the woman gives birth to a child, once again her name changes. Now she is the mother of "Y". This grants her full status of woman, and assures her place in the community. Failure to bear children means possible ostracism by the husband and community. At some point, the husband might either send her away or marry again.[20]

If a woman eventually becomes a grandmother, with a long and successful lineage, she is conferred almost all the status of a man. She can attend men's meetings and is greatly respected throughout the community. At this point, if she is too old to work in the fields, children and grandchildren take care of her.[21]

Although often respected in the community, women had few legal rights prior to 1980. For example, in the event of a divorce, the husband kept the children born from the marriage. A wife was only allowed to keep a child still nursing. If the husband died, the wife still was not entitled to the children, and could easily be inherited by one of her deceased husband's brothers. If she had a son, he retained all of the property and, if old enough, became her guardian. Thus, in a legal sense, she was a minor "from cradle to grave."[22] Because of her minor status, she could not even file for divorce; she had to enlist the help of her father or former guardian. This was not always forthcoming, however, because the father would have to refund a portion of the brideprice, depending on how many children were born.[23]

In the salaried sector, women's status was not much improved in the years before black majority rule. As soon as a woman married, she was put on temporary staff. Her income was heavily taxed, as it was not considered as important as her husband's. If she became pregnant, she was forced to resign and reapply after the birth of her child.[24]

In studies of urban women, few know their husband's actual earnings, and most only receive allowances. Their husbands encourage them to work both inside and outside the home, but having less education means they are usually relegated to menial tasks.[25]

Legal remedies after 1980

With the advent of the Mugabe administration, legal enactments were supposed to guarantee women the same rights as men. Some were more successful than others, and included:

1) The Legal Age of Majority Act, late 1982. This was probably the most significant enactment pertaining to the government's goal of equality for men and women. The law did away with women's legal status as a minor as soon as she reached eighteen. This was supposed to be a truly revolutionary law for Zimbabwean women. They now had the power to sue and be sued, own property, and most important of all, enter a contract of marriage without their father's consent or exchange of brideprice. This also allowed women to become guardians of their own children.[26] The tradition of brideprice still persists, however, particularly in rural areas, and it will no doubt be some time before it dies out completely.

As exemplified in the view of one writer, "What the law says is one thing; practice is another. For most women today...the act might as well not exist. There is hardly any change at all." Women are so set in their ways, she states, they could never imagine being men's equals. Many are actually against the provisions of the act. There is still the prevailing view among men and women that if large amounts of brideprice were paid then the wife has very little she can say or do without her husband's permission.[27]

2) *The Matrimonial Causes Act, 1985.* This legislation permitted the court to divide up the property accumulated by the wife in any way the court decides instead of it being the sole property of the man.[28]

3) *The Labor Relations Act, 1986.* Women were entitled to 90 days paid maternity leave, and they should be offered the same position at the same salary after her delivery. All other benefits should continue uninterrupted.

This latter act, along with mandated minimum wage increases in occupations dominated by women, is certainly paved with good intentions. However, it does make women relatively more expensive than previously, which may increase their likelihood of being laid off or not hired in the first place.

In spite of these progressive actions, Zimbabwean women are still do not have one of the most important institutional rights. They are not allowed to own land. This is the norm in sub-Saharan Africa, and is rationalized as being the 'African tradition.' If a man who is 'the head' of the family dies, his wife and children may be forced to leave their home. The man's brothers and relatives have claim to all his land and all his possessions. As late as 1998, Joseph Msika, the government minister in charge of land resettlement, rejected women's demands for land permits to be automatically registered in the names of both spouses. His reason was simple- he claimed it would lead to the break-up of homes.[29]

Given this legal environment, the land reform movement was implicitly aimed at helping black male Zimbabweans. The end result was that both men and women were hurt by the land seizures, but women were hurt disproportionately more, since they are more likely to engage in informal and agricultural activities. Although legal gains had been made for women during the 1980s, the land seizures countered the economic ones, and in doing so hurt an extremely productive share of Zimbabwe's labor force.

Chapter 8. Lessons Learned From Nicaragua, Consequences, and Conclusions

There are few cases in history where a country with so much promise has been thrown off the rails with such abandon. This makes it difficult to gamely suggest a path out of Zimbabwe's current mess. It appears intractable. However, there is another country that endured a highly similar tragedy, and it is worth investigating that case as a beacon of hope and a roadmap for Zimbabwe's recovery in this final chapter.

Some Intriguing Parallels with Nicaragua

The plight and resulting crash of Zimbabwe's economy is eerily similar to a country halfway around the world. That country is Nicaragua. Like Zimbabwe, Nicaragua was a country whose strong economic growth largely benefited the rich elite landholders. The Somoza dictatorship was in no hurry to redistribute income, and this created the opportunity for a Communist revolutionary named Daniel Ortega. From 1977 to 1979 Ortega led a bloody revolution, which ultimately led to the rise in power of his Sandinista political party. Like Mugabe's ZANU-PF party, the Sandinistas had ridden in on the politically popular issue of land reform, and in July of 1979 a new decree allowed the Sandinista party to begin confiscating property belonging to Somoza. The vague wording and lax application of the decree allowed Sandinista officials to confiscate property from any "follower" of Somoza. Through the early 1980s, the newly formed Ministry of Agricultural Development and Agrarian Reform (MIDINRA) seized farm after farm, totaling nearly a quarter of all the arable land. As Everingham (2001) noted, "The popular stampede toward land ownership trampled heavily on the property rights of a privileged but divided elite."[1] Other decrees soon followed, allowing members of the party to take "abandoned" property, unused urban property and companies whose management was thought to be "de-capitalizing" the enterprise. Eventually the Sandinistas seized 34 percent of all arable land.[2]

Probably to satisfy the critics, the Sandinista regime promised compensation and due process from the former landholders, though in practice these measures were applied informally and often without proper landowner compensation. Like Zimbabwe, the government officials took the farms first, and only later doled out remaining farms for individual peasants. The documentation handling the land transfers was poorly handled and administered. As a result, more than 70 percent of the land grants were legally suspect, and thus lost much of their equity value. After eleven years in power, the Sandinista government had confiscated about 170,000 properties, including many that were seized right before the Chamorro government assumed power. Yet only 55,000 households had received private titles, which were of questionable security.[3]

Like Zimbabwe, the land seizures and disregard for property rights in general led to similar disastrous economic consequences. Along with land seizures, private banks and other companies were taken over by the government, using coercion when necessary. Over its reign, the Sandinista government ended up inefficiently running 351 enterprises, which consumed nearly a third of the economy. Not surprisingly, ordinary Nicaraguans' wealth and income plummeted. During the first three years of the revolution (1977-1979), per-capita income fell by over 35 percent. By 1990, per-capita income had slipped to half of what it was prior to the arrival of the Sandinistas.[4] Part of this was also due to economic sanctions from the United States and a bloody war with rebel forces.

Yet clearly the wealth-destroying effect of land and bank seizures had ruined the trust and confidence in the Nicaraguan economy, both domestically and worldwide. This led to a similar domino effect that ultimately destroyed the currency's value, and with it, Nicaraguan's hopes and savings for the future. Inflation skyrocketed out of control during the late 1980s, as government spending soared and the central bank printed money to cover the deficits. At its worst, prices grew at an annual rate of more than 13,000 percent.[5] This is illustrated in Table 8.1 below.

Table 8.1. Nicaragua: Inflation and GDP growth, 1984-2000

Year	Inflation Rate	Real GDP growth
1984	35.4	-1.6
1985	219.5	-4.1
1986	681.6	-1.0
1987	912.0	-0.7
1988	14,316.0	-12.4
1989	4,770.0	-1.7
1990	12,338.0	0.0
1991	775.0	-0.2
1992	32.5	0.4
1993	20.4	-0.4
1994	19.6	3.3
1995	20.0	4.3
1996	12.6	4.5
1997	7.3	5.0
1998	8.0	4.8
1999	6.5	5.3
2000	5.0	5.7

Source: Selected statistics come from Everingham (2001), who used statistics from the Interamerican Development Bank (IDB), Statistics and Quantitative Analysis Unit, *Nicaragua Country Report (2000)*, based in Washington, DC. Other statistics were obtained from USAID Latin American and Caribbean division, selected statistics, 1996.

By 1990, Nicaragua was in shambles. The Sandinista government agreed to hold democratic elections, and Violeta Barrios de Chamorro was democratically elected that year, representing centrist views. Through the next five years, the Chamorro government turned Nicaragua's course around in a remarkable way. Williams (1994) noted that the new democracy rested squarely on the process of restoring property rights.[6] The "support" provided by the United States was initially channeled through USAID and then placed under the strict tutelage of the IMF; the U.S. refused to pardon any debt. The Barrios de Chamorro administration had no choice but to accept the IMF position in order to gain access to further funds. In response to the IMF directives, the government re-established the role of private banks and redefined the role of the state commercial banks and the central bank.[7]

The IMF directives also led to the central bank clamping down on the money supply. The results were dramatic. From 1991 to 1992, the inflation rate plummeted from 766 percent to only eight percent. In addition to putting the screws to hyperinflation, the government moved towards freeing up the marketplace. It dismantled trading monopolies, permitted the reemergence of private banking, sold off state enterprises and reformed tax and trade laws.

Furthermore, it has continued to exercise monetary and fiscal constraint. Unlike Chile, which took seven years to reduce most tariffs from 90 percent to 10 percent, Nicaragua dropped tariffs from an average of 200 percent in 1989 to 43 percent in 1990 and to 15 percent in 1991. The efforts paid off, saving the economy from collapse, but still it continued to contract, albeit at a far slower rate.

In 1992 the Chamorro government turned full attention towards its most difficult task yet-a comprehensive rehabilitation of property rights. Perhaps the most important signal to the marketplace both domestically and abroad was the resolve of the Nicaraguan government to increase the trust in its institutions, through devoting tremendous resources towards properly titling land. It did this through the founding (in late 1991) of The Nicaraguan Institute of Agrarian

Reform (INRA), which served as a component of the National Program of Land Measurement, Titling and Registration. Between 1992 and 1996 INRA provided technical support in the legal reconsideration of 10,500 titles that had been seized by the Sandinista administration from private individuals. Together, these holdings encompassed 615,000 hectares of land. Perhaps not coincidentally, it was in 1992 when the GDP slowly began its upturn, and by 1993 the economy was nosing towards positive economic growth for the first time in eight years, as seen in Figure 8.1 below. From 1993 on, the economy moved strongly upwards, edging towards nearly 6% growth by the late 1990s. This marked it as one of the strongest growing countries in the world.

All is not sanguine, however. The issue of restoring property rights continues to be a difficult one. While the confiscation of property was highly popular in some quarters during the Sandinista years, now former property owners want compensation or the return of their land. To settle these disputes, the value of the land is determined by INRA, and the resulting compensation to the owners is paid out in bonds that mature in fifteen years. The bonds trade for about twenty cents on the dollar, so former owners get far less than the value of their lost property.[8] Most Nicaraguans did not trust waiting fifteen years to be paid, and sold their bonds immediately, getting what they could for their property.[9] This is not surprising considering their country's past with hyperinflation. With more than 160,000 rural households still having title disputes in 2002, the government was still overflowing with legal challenges.[10] As Everingham (2001) put it, "constitutional reform resulted in rampant legal ambiguity rather than solid institutional stability."[11]

As an example, *The New York Times* in September 2000 related the story of how one cattle farmer, Emilio Aguilar, was forced off his ranch after being declared a counterrevolutionary in 1979 by the Sandinista government. He returned in 1991 to demand compensation from the Chamorro government, but turned down their offer of low value 15-year bonds. Instead, he said he was intent on suing the mayors who gave away his land. Indeed, the courthouse now resides right in the middle of his former farm.[12]

Figure 8.1. Nicaragua: GDP Growth Rates 1984-2000

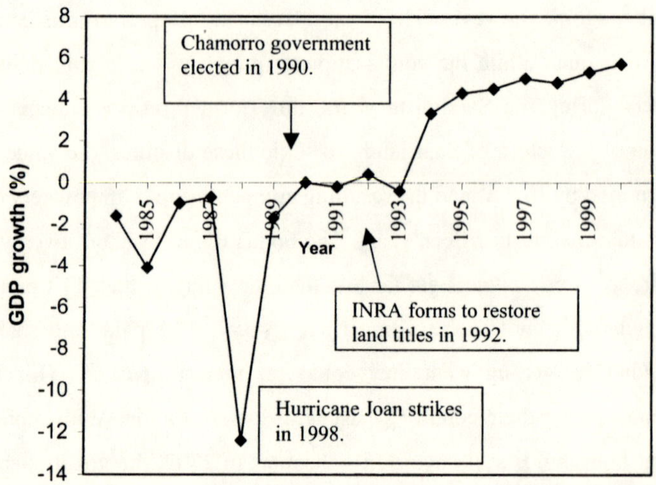

Source: Table 8.1

Resolving these complex and competing property claims is now the biggest hurdle to attracting foreign investment in what is still the Western Hemisphere's second poorest nation (Haiti is at bottom). Lino Hernandez, president of the Permanent Commission of Human Rights of Nicaragua, stated that "if there is no solution to the property question, there will be no security or investment in this country. Ten years have passed and we feel powerless that we cannot find a solution to this problem."[13]

Nicaragua indeed has a tough slog ahead. Although it posted strong economic growth, its population is increasing at a 3 percent rate, which has done little to raise average Nicaraguan's incomes.[14] This is not an unusual side effect of "cold-shower" reform efforts. Often there is a delay in the positive impacts. Bolivia, for example, initiated its structural adjustment in 1985. Not until the 1990s was this belt-tightening considered to have had a positive impact in terms of economic growth (though its impact on poverty appears to be minimal, as in similar cases in Peru and El Salvador). Poland's economic reforms also took some time to turn its economy around.[15]

Nicaragua has also had plenty of help to get it off its feet. Between 1990 and 1993, foreign aid donations and concessional loans were equal to nearly half of Nicaragua's gross domestic product. These funds help Nicaragua to finance its relatively large deficits. Today, Nicaragua has a debt-to-GDP ratio higher than any other country in the world except Guyana. In 1994, Nicaragua paid US$238 million (13 percent of GDP, 79 percent of the FOB export value) to service external debt. Nicaragua's current debt was still staggering, however; at US$12 billion, it was the equivalent of fifty years of current export earnings.[16] And since that time, the international donor community has contributed another $4 billion.[17]

However, by 1998 Nicaragua had "made substantial progress in reducing economic imbalances and moving toward a market-based economy," according to an IMF report. Its overall fiscal balance had greatly improved, inflation was sharply down, and GDP growth up.[18] Since that time, Nicaragua still struggles with its high debt, and resolving property rights claims, but it is making progress. Based on its continuing commitment towards protecting property rights and free markets, one can be cautiously optimistic about its future. This story also illustrates that markets can be rebuilt even after their bedrock institutions are heavily damaged.

The Consequences of Insecure Property Rights

Around the world people continue to debate the importance of property rights, in spite of evidence and common sense that says if one doesn't allow people the gains of their industry, they will not work. We have also seen how a network of wealth develops when property titles allow an owner to leverage his property into loans for other items. Both of these mechanisms serve as the crucial linchpins for allowing and spurring economic growth. Unfortunately, politically hungry leaders seize upon the seductive but ill-founded notion that damaging property rights is a cheap way of distributing wealth from a "less deserving" group to a "more deserving" group.

We have seen in this book the extremely severe consequences of those actions. Who was hurt the most? In general, the "more deserving group" was. White commercial farmers have left for other places, having to start from scratch, but they took with them their knowledge of how to live far beyond a subsistence level. Blacks on the other hand, stay in Zimbabwe- impoverished, starving and witnessing the deaths of their loved ones at an early age.

Yet many places around the world ignore the lessons of Zimbabwe. In January 2004, fifteen thousand squatters occupied farmers' lands in Gabon, South Africa, claiming that the farmers had plenty of extra land to go around.

As one resident squatter said, "We've got a right to be here. The owner wasn't using this land." Lately, the farmers are seeing less regard for the law. Police demanded $250,000 from one farmer to clear the squatters off the land. In addition, The Landless People's Movement, a fast-growing political group in South Africa, hopes to start taking over white farms in early 2005, at the climax of the presidential election season. Says organizer Magaliso Kubheka, ''we are going to shake them."[19]

Unfortunately, out of three-dozen countries in Africa, two-thirds have either stagnated or shrunk in real per capita terms since the onset of independence in the early 1960s. Millions of dollars spent in international aid to aid in free market reforms failed. They failed because these countries lacked a limit on government power, and they lacked government secured property rights.[20]

Even the Western world is susceptible. The Netherlands is renowned for its prowess as a global trader, and embraces free markets and property rights. Yet a specific type of squatting is fully legal in this country; under Dutch law any vacant building is up for grabs, including government buildings such as schools or administration offices. As a result, landlords have to solicit professional "anti-squatters" from reputable companies to live in vacant buildings and keep out the squatters, creating inefficiencies in the marketplace.[21] Fortunately, these types of laws are a nuisance rather than a serious blow to Dutch property rights.

Room for Optimism: A Roadmap for the Future

With so many things going wrong in Zimbabwe, it is easy to forget how many assets this country has. Despite being landlocked, it has thousands of acres of rich farmland, and billions of dollars worth of precious metals and other natural resources. Its population is well educated, and generally respects the rule of law, with crime rates only slightly higher than the United States.[22] Zimbabwe's government institutions were based on the United States' system, with executive, legislative and judicial branches each having separately defined and limiting powers. The central bank was modeled after the Federal Reserve. The press, until recently, enjoyed a measure of freedom in criticizing the government, and was read by a large number of citizens. Zimbabwe has an airline company, power companies, decent roads, and gorgeous nature preserves.

At the same time, Zimbabwe's potential for economic growth has been stymied over the past twenty years by Mugabe's socialist ZANU-PF government. As we have seen, the government's grossly inefficient policies led to nationalization of many industries, subsidization of others, distortions in foreign exchange markets, an explosion of the money supply, rampant deficits, and of course more recently, a trampling of democratic freedoms and property rights. All of this has deeply shaken the trust of both Zimbabwe's citizens and the world abroad. It is no wonder that direct foreign investment, once a healthy 440 billion U.S. dollars in 1998, plummeted to one percent of that level by the year 2003.

Given that the Mugabe government has damaged so many of its important institutions and resources, Zimbabwe now faces what Stephen Haber and Douglas North once called the "thorny" problem. That is, a new government needs to be strong enough to enforce property rights and rule of law, but not so overbearing as to constrict the marketplace.[23] The good news is that underneath Zimbabwe's suffocating policies is a strong democratic structure that can potentially support and nourish free markets. The challenge, then, is to find ways to restore faith and security in property rights, while at the same time sharply limit the current government interference in the free market. As Milton Friedman (1962) wrote:

> What the market does is reduce greatly the range of issues that must be decided through political means, and thereby minimize the extent to which the government need participate directly in the game... Economic strength becomes a check to political power rather than reinforcement.[24]

When issues are decided by economic means, there are nearly always more efficient results and far more productive activity. Here, then, are eight concrete proposals that seek to expand the role of the free market in Zimbabwe. These proposals do not require loans from international lending institutions, nor do they cost much money to implement. Rather, they work by bringing to life Zimbabwe's enormous yet hidden potential for economic growth and prosperity, potential that has been buried under a sea of government regulations and operations.

Policy Proposals

1. Restore agricultural property rights and provide government resources to enforce them.

The government, in the wake of the 2000-2003 land reforms, is now the owner of thousands of acres of former commercial farmland. Individuals apply to lease tiny plots of land on a year-to-year basis, and are vulnerable to non-renewal at any time. These individuals have no title to the land, and no sense of ownership. Predictably, this has led to a tremendous drop in agricultural production, poor land management, and an enormous destruction of wealth in the economy. In the name of fairness, Mugabe's policies have now made nearly everyone poor. Individual farmers see little point to improving or taking care of land that might not be theirs next year. Billions of dollars worth of equity, so vital for borrowing and investing, have been lost since the government took ownership of the land.

How to proceed? Despite the challenges Zimbabwe faces, the case of Nicaragua, as discussed earlier, is an instructive one. After the demise of the Sandinista socialist regime, we saw how the pro-market Chamorro government formed a government-titling agency that was the key component to jump-starting the Nicaraguan economic engine. Only a year later, a once sputtering economy leaped up to 3-4 percent annual GDP growth.

Zimbabwe needs to follow suit, and issue land titles to individuals interested in investing in the development of small-scale commercial farmland, in place of leasing the land on an annual basis. Currently, there are thousands of small-scale commercial farms already in existence in Zimbabwe. Nearly all are black-owned, so they serve as an important psychological symbol to black Zimbabweans. These farms demonstrate that blacks can be successful farmers, and are not simply doomed to subsistence farming methods, as the stereotype runs. The land is generally well managed, commercially successful, and titled, enabling these farmers to get loans from banks for seeds, fertilizer and the like. These small-scale commercial farming techniques can also restore the productivity of the heavily degraded communal lands, which suffer from the tragedy of the commons.

2. Let export companies keep their hard currency profits rather than surrendering them to the Zimbabwean government.

Currently export companies must surrender most, if not all of their hard currency earnings to the government; in exchange they receive Zimbabwean dollars at the official exchange rate, which is far below the parallel, or "street" rate of exchange. This desperate and myopic policy has been an attempt by the government to stave off bankruptcy, as Zimbabwean dollars become increasingly worthless. The problem is that export companies are dependent upon their hard currency earnings to purchase imported inputs such as fuel and parts. As a result, they find themselves in an increasingly untenable condition. As we saw in Chapter 5, a dozen gold mines shut down in 2003 alone, dropping Zimbabwe from third to eighth place in worldwide gold production.

The rare success story, however, is platinum, which is one of the few growth industries in Zimbabwe. (Projections by analysts claim that Zimbabwe is now believed to have one of the largest reserves in the world.) The difference between gold and platinum production is simple: Gold mines are forced to turn over most of their hard currency earnings, whereas platinum mines face no such restriction. As a result, financial capital is flowing into Zimbabwe from all over the world to develop platinum mines, even as once profitable gold mines close.

By using the platinum mines as a model for all export companies, Zimbabwe's vast economic potential can be realized. The expanding commercial operations will also provide an important source of tax revenue for the government, assuming corporate income taxes are lowered.

3. Drastically lower corporate income taxes, as well as import duties.

Currently corporate income taxes are 37.5 percent. Branches of foreign corporations are subject to an additional tax of 8.4 percent. Import duties range up to more than 100 percent.[25]

In an interesting experiment, several years ago Zimbabwe established "Export Processing Zones" (EPZs) that were designed to encourage companies to invest in these areas, somewhat like free enterprise zones in the United States. The benefits for locating there include duty-free imports used for raw materials, and a series of tax breaks. The only drawback is a statute requiring these companies to export at least 80 percent of their output, presumably so the government can earn more hard currency. This requirement has substantially slowed down investment in this area.

Zimbabwe would also do well to follow the example of Ireland, formerly one of the poorest countries in Europe. Now known as the "Celtic tiger", Ireland lowered its countrywide corporate income tax rate to a flat ten percent in the mid-1990s, feeling it had little to lose. As a result, entrepreneurial activity soared. Billions of dollars of foreign investment soon followed, as well as booming economic growth.[26] It is now the healthiest economy in Europe. If Zimbabwe drops the 80 percent export rule, and expands the Export Processing Zone to include the entire country, Zimbabwe would be on its way to becoming an "African tiger."

4. Re-institute the independence of the Reserve Bank of Zimbabwe's from the Treasury department.

Zimbabwe's Treasury and Reserve Bank once had united policies of keeping inflation and unemployment low. In case after case, it has been shown that the most important way to stimulate long-term employment is to focus on stabilizing the money supply, thereby keeping inflation in check. Internally, that is still the Reserve Bank's official goal, but it has been thwarted by the Mugabe government's insistence that the Bank buy up the increasingly worthless Treasury securities. This practice needs to be stopped, in order to restore faith in the workings of Zimbabwe's monetary system, and end the spiraling hyperinflation.

5. End the attacks on the free press and competing political parties.

Western journalists should be invited back into the country, to chronicle the changes in the economy and government. This will enhance the credibility of the government and reassure financial markets.

6. Privatize the government-owned businesses, and deregulate all price and wage controls.

As has been discussed in this book, the government is suffering enormous losses in many of its publicly owned operations, with the losses from the Grain Marketing Board alone claiming a 1.5 percent share of GDP. These operations should be sold to the private sector, which will lower deficits, and result in far more efficient production methods. Funds from the public auctions of these companies can be used to restore publicly maintained resources, such as roads and schools.

7. Issue compensation to displaced white commercial farmers.

As in Nicaragua, a poor country like Zimbabwe would have a difficult time paying the full market value of commercial farmland to the displaced farmers. However, by making some payment, the government of Zimbabwe would send an important message to its citizens as well as potential foreign investors. The message would be that Zimbabwe fundamentally respects the rule of law, particularly with regard to property rights. Recall that by Zimbabwean law, white commercial farmers were supposed to be compensated, but in practice this has rarely happened. Instead, the Mugabe government has brusquely ignored the laws. By compensating farmers at least some amount, this would show government's good faith, and go a long way towards reassuring worldwide financial markets.

8. Ask for forgiveness of debt from international lending agencies.

This should be contingent upon Zimbabwe's rigorous attention to following the steps 1 through 8 outlined above.

Zimbabwe, a land of so much potential, has the capability to bloom once again given the right circumstances. Those circumstances, as we have seen, require the restoring of secure property rights as the key first step. From there, Zimbabwe can move towards building economic growth and prosperity for its entire people.

Chapter notes

Introduction.

[1] Information for points 1-5, 7 and 8,9 comes from the July 2003 IMF Country Report, "Zimbabwe: Selected Issues and Statistical Appendix". Point 6 is from The Heritage Foundation Freedom Index. I thank Arthur Goldsmith of UMass Boston College of Management and Barrie Richardson (emeritus) of Centenary College for their extremely helpful comments and observations in this section.

[2] See Alwang, et.al, and Ross, et. al.

[3] Unattributed, "Zimbabwe to name thousands of blacks to get farms of whites." *New York Times*, Dec. 30, 2001.

[4] July 2003 IMF Country report, p. 26

[5] According to the OECD (2003) and the IMF, other sectors of GDP include: manufacturing, 18-20 percent of the economy (60 percent of which is devoted to agriculture); hotels and restaurants, 18%, transport storage and communications, 9%; finance and insurance, 9%, public administration, 3%; construction, 3%, mining, 4%, real estate, 4% and other, roughly 16%.

[6] IMF Country Report 03/225- "Zimbabwe: Selected Issues." (July 2003), p. 26.

[7] This number is estimated using the process described on page 84 of this book.

[8] *World Development Indicators for Zimbabwe.* The World Bank, 2002.

Chapter one

[1] *The Economist*, "It's The King's Land, OK?" Dec. 31, 1999.

[2] Wilson, Derek. *The World Encompassed.* Harper and Row: New York. 1977

[3] Goldsmith, p. 5.

[4] La Porta, Rafael, Lopez-de-Silanes, Forencio, Shleifer, Andreiand Vishny, Robert W. "Law and Finance", *Journal of Political Economy*, 106/6 (1998) pp. 1113-55.

[5] See de Soto, *The Mystery of Capital*, Chapter 5.

[6], Torstennson, Johan, "Property rights and Economic Growth: An empirical study," *Kyklos*, 1994, Vol. 47, Issue 2.

[7] See Campbell, John L. and Leon Lindberg, "Property Rights and The Organization of Economic Activity By The State." *American Sociological Review*, Oct. 1990; Block, Fred, 1986, "Political Choice and Multiple 'Logics' of Capital" *Theory and Society* 15:175-92 and Granovetter, Mark, 1985, "Economic Action and Social Structure: The Problem of Embeddedness" *American Journal of Sociology* 91: 481-510.

[8] Norton, Seth. "Poverty, Property Rights, and Human Well-Being: A Cross-National Study." *CATO Journal*, Fall98, Vol. 18, Issue 2
[9] Knight (1971: 319)
[10] Erica Field, "Entitled to Work: Urban Property Rights and Labor Supply in Peru, Economics Department, Princeton University, 2002 (unpublished.)
[11] de Soto, p. 253.
[12] de Soto, p. 21.
[13] de Soto, p. 61.
[14] World Bank (1999): Country Brief: Nicaragua, May 1999. Http://wbln0018.worldbank.org
[15] This framework is abbreviated by the full "taxonomy" laid out by Kunkhlande and Luckert; I chose what I believed to be the most significant ones affecting Zimbabwe and economies in general.
[16] de Soto discusses this in the case of American squatters in the 1800s in *Mystery of Capital.*

Chapter two

[17] Sylvester, p. 16.
[18] ibid, p. 17.
[19] ibid, p. 17.
[20] ibid, p. 16.
[21] ibid, p.119.
[22] *Zimbabwe Country Profile, 1988-89, p. 3.*
[23] Sylvester, p. 37.
[24] ibid, p. 41.
[25] ibid, p. 42.
[26] ibid, p. 46.
[27] Gann and Henriksen, p. 66.
[28] Country Watch.com, Zimbabwe Political history.
[29] Economist Intelligence Unit (1989), p. 4.
[30] Skalnes, p. 97.
[31] Dashwood, Hevina, *Zimbabwe: The Political Economy of Transformation*, p. 26-28.
[32] Country Watch.com.
[33] Dashwood, p. 28.
[34] Skalnes, p 160.
[35] ibid, p. 160.
[36] *New African Yearbook*, "Political History of Zimbabwe". 1998. (internet site).
[37] Country Watch. com.
[38] *The Economist*, p. 21.
[39] Skalnes, p. 160.
[40] ibid, p. 161.
[41] ibid, p. 161.
[42] ibid, p. 161.
[43] ibid, p. 161.
[44] *New African Yearbook.*
[45] *New African Yearbook.*
[46] Skalnes, p. 164.
[47] ibid.
[48] ibid.
[49] *British Embassy*. "The UK and Zimbabwe." Department for International Development, April 2003.
[50] Zeilig, Leo, "Crisis in Zimbabwe." *International Socialism Journal*, Issue 94, Spring 2002.
[51] ibid.
[52] *British Embassy*, ibid.

[53] ibid.
[54] IRINNEWS.org, "MDC set to challenge election result." April 10, 2002.
[55] ibid.
[56] July 2003 IMF report, p. 25.
[57] Source: e-mail correspondence with Neil Wright, chief economist for the Commercial Farmer's Union., 10/28/03.
[58] United Nations Office, IRIN.org. "Zimbabwe: By-election marred by allegations of foul play.", Oct. 28, 2002, www.irinnews.org/report.asp
[59] *Africa News Service*, "WFP Warns of Disaster in Zimbabwe, Dec. 7, 2002.
[60] Chitepo, Witness, "Zimbabwe: Rushing backwards," in *African Business*, Sept. 2002
[61] ibid.
[62] ibid.
[63] *African News Service*, Dec. 7, 2002.
[64] The Media Institute of Southern Africa wrote an open letter to Kofi Annan which condemned the treatment of Zimbabwe journalists by Mugabe's government, which has increased the increasing restrictions on what may be broadcast. See www.misanet.org/zimprotest/letters/UN.html.
[65] IRINNEWS.org. "Bombing of radio office condemned." August, 29, 2002.
[66] Glaser, Mark, "Zimbabwe's Daily News Fights Closure with Online Publication." *USC Annenberg Online Journalism Review*. 10/22/2003. Available at: http://www.ojr.org/ojr/glaser/1066860746.php. In addition, unattributed author, INDEX (online) "Zimbabwe: Daily News still closed despite appeal ruling" available at: http://www.indexonline.org/indexindex/20030918_zimbabwe.shtml
[67] Thurow, Roger "Once a Breadbasket, Zimbabwe Today Can't Feed Itself," *Wall Street Journal,* December 24, 2003 p. A1.
[68] Unattributed, "Victory for Daily News" in Zimbabwe's *Daily News* online edition, Jan. 4, 2004.
[69] Willmer, Tanya, "Commonwealth policy on Zim in tatters" in iafrica.com, available at: http://iafrica.com/news/specialreport/zimbabwe/290397.htm
[70] Unattributed, *The Commonwealth of Learning* (official website of the Commonwealth), available at: www.col.org.
[71] IRINNEWS.org, "EU names Zimbabwe's blacklist", July 25, 2002.
[72] Friedman, Milton. *Capitalism and Freedom (1962)*
[73] House, p. 19, 20.
[74] ibid, p. 22.

Chapter three

[1] E-mail correspondence with Neil Wright, chief economist for CFU, 10/28/03.
[2] da Silva, Vicky, "The Land Issue in Zimbabwe" Electoral Institute of Southern Africa,, eisa.org.za., Feb. 25, 2002.
[3] July 2003 IMF 03/225 report, p.18.
[4] Mumbengegwi, p. 209.
[5] ibid, p. 210.
[6] Mumbengegwi, p. 212.
[7] Billing, p. 21.
[8] World Bank, *Trends in Developing Economies*, p. 13.
[9] Economist Intelligence Unit (1989), p. 15.
[10] Economist Intelligence Unit (1989), p. 15.
[11] Billing, p. 20.
[12] Skalnes p. 101.
[13] Hill, Ryan, and Katarere, Yemi. "Colonialism and Inequity in Zimbabwe." IUCN report: Harare. 2001.

[14] Bate, Roger, "Culling to be kind," *The Competitive Enterprise Institute*, March 16, 1999. Available at http://www.cei.org/gencon/004,01572.cfm
[15] Ryan, ibid.
[16] Godwin, Peter, "A Land Possessed," *National Geographic*, August 2003.
[17] Nyambara, Pius Shugudzapera, "The Politics of Land Acquisition and Struggles Over Land in the 'Communal' Areas of Zimbabwe: The Gokwe Region in the 1980s and 1990s. Africa 71 (2), 2001, and Baker, J. Rural Communities Under Stress: peasant farmers and the state in Africa. Cambridge: Cambridge University Press. 1989 and Moyo, Sam. *The Land Question in Zimbabwe* 1995. Harare: SAPES.
[18] Nyambara, p. 266.
[19] Kundhlande, G. and M.K. Luckert, "Towards an Analytical Framework for Assessing Property Rights to Natural Resources: A Case Study in the Communal Areas of Zimbabwe. Staff Paper, Department of Rural Economy, University of Alberta.
[20] Bruce, J.W., L. Fortmann, and C. Nhira. 1993. "Tenures in Transition, Tenures in Conflict: Examples for the Zimbabwean Social Forest". *Rural Sociology* 54 (4): 626-42.
[21] Kundhlande.
[22] World Bank, *Zimbabwe Population Sector Report*, Main Report, p. 12.
[23] ibid.
[24] See Stephen Prince's work and more Landsat photos at the Department of Geography, The University of Maryland, at www.geog.umd.edu/LGRSS/Projects/zimbabwe
[25] Source for above table: Billing, p. 20; Moyo, p. 188; and World Bank "Land Subsector Study", p. 12, 13.
[26] IMF report, July 2003, p. 18
[27] In an inaugural meeting in April 2002 of the African Ministerial Conference on Water, David Grey, the Senior Water Advisor of the World Bank described the integral role that water plays in Africa's economic development in a speech titled "Water Resources and Poverty in Africa: Breaking the Vicious Circle", based on a paper written by Grey and Cludia Sadoff.
[28] See Stiglitz, Joseph. *Globalization and its Discontents* (2003). Norton and Company: New York. This somewhat parallels the case of England, which did the same with the "hard influence" of armies and naval fleets during the reign of the British empire, as detailed in Empire, by Niall Ferguson.

Chapter four

[1] Skalines, p. 165.
[2] ibid, p. 165.
[3] *Economist Intelligence Unit*, p. 17.
[4] ibid, p. 15.
[5] ibid, p. 17.
[6] Skalines, from World Bank figures, p. 172.
[7] *Economist Intelligence Unit* (1990), p. 21.
[8] Ministry of Finance, *Socioeconomic Review*, p. 86,87.
[9] Economist Intelligence Unit (1989), p. 30.
[10] Skalnes, p. 171.
[11] ibid, p. 177.
[12] Sachikonye, L.M. "Industrial Restructuring and Labour Relations" in *Structural Adjustment and the Working Poor in Zimbabwe*, edited by Peter Gibbon, p. 98.
[13] Bijlmakers, L. et. al. "Heath and Structural Adjustment in Rural and Urban Settings in Zimbabwe. Some Interim Findings.", in Structural Adjustment and the Working Poor in Zimbabwe, edited by Peter Gibbon. Nordiska Africkinstitutet: Uppsala.
[14] World Bank, Report no. P1C1101, "Zimbabwe-Structural Adjustment Loan III, internal report, 1994.
[15] Alwang, Jeffery, et. al. "Why Has Poverty Increased in Zimbabwe?", World Bank: March

2002.
16 Sachikonye, p. 109.
17 ibid, p. 118.
18 ibid, p. 127.
19 World Bank, Zimbabwe: Article IV, p. 5 (box)
20 Lee, Richard. "Crisis in Chidobe," in *Zimbabwe Eyewitness*, World Food Program, at www.wfp.org/newsroom/in_depth/africa/sa_chidobe0209.htm
21 *FASonline*. "Zimbabwe: Drought Threatens 2001/02 Summer Crops." February 20, 2002, at http://www.fas.usda.gov/pecad2/highlights/2002/02/zim/zimfeb.htm
22 *Food and Agricultural Organization*. "Special Report: FAO/WFP Crop and Food Supply Assessment Mission to Zimbabwe." May 29th, 2002, pp. 1-3, at http://www.fao.org/docrep/005/y6816e/y6816e00.htm
23 ibid, p. 6.
24 See http://www.sadc-fanr.org.zw/zw/zwcul1e.htm for a view of the crop zones.
25 FAO Special Report, p. 6.
26 *ReliefWeb*, "Zimbabwe: Drought takes toll on livestock", April 8, 2003.
27 See Natsios, Andrew, Administrator for USAID in "The Food Crisis in Southern Africa: The Challenge to Sustainability," reported at a Foreign Press Briefing, on August 20, 2002, and Zimbabwe's *Daily News*, "Bulawayo City Council rules out water rationing." where Zimbabwe's dams were reported as 74 percent full by Peter Sibanda, Bulawayo's Director of Engineering Services. He said there was enough water to last through the next rainy season.
28 Natsios, ibid. p. 2.
29 July 2003 IMF report, ,Table II.1. Maize production, p. 19.
30 WFP Eyewitness, "Crisis in Chidobe." September 2002.
31 Dempster, Carolyn, "Zimbabwe's Changed Land" at *BBC News*, http://news.bbc.co.uk, Feb. 28, 2003.
32 Information provided by Neil Wright, economist at CFU via e-mail, 10/28/03 .
33 Godwin, Peter, "Land Possessed." *National Geographic*, August 2003.
34 FAO/WFP Crop and Food Supply Assessment Mission to Zimbabwe, May 29, 2002, p. 7.
35 Dempster, Carolyn. "Zimbabwe's Changed Land."
36 ibid.
37 Godwin, Peter, "Land Possessed." *National Geographic*, August 2003.
38 Wines, Michael, "A Bleak Ride Home for Zimbabwe Deportees." *The New York Times*, Sept 23, 2003 pA1 col 01.
39 Godwin, Peter, ibid.
40 World Bank. "Economics of Tobacco Control", at http://www1.worldbank.org/tobacco/chapter5.asp
41 FAO/WFP report, under "Yields" section.
42 Information provided by Neil Wright, economist at CFU via e-mail, 10/28/03.
43 FAO/WFP report, under "Area Planted" section.
44 OECD Report: Zimbabwe, pp.1-3.
45 Godwin, Peter, ibid.
46 July IMF report, p. 26.

Chapter five

47 July 2003 IMF report., p 20.
48 ibid
49 ibid.
50 ibid.
51 ibid, p. 11.
52 ibid, p. 12.
53 *Economist* "Zimbabwe's Beans and Bicycles", 2/17/2001.

[54] *African Business*, October 2001.
[55] *Pana Daily News Wire*. "Zimbabwe's Central Bank tightens Foreign exchange rules." 11/25/2001
[56] *Financial Gazette*. "The Costs of Parallel Exchange Rates", 1/17/2002.
[57] July 2003 IMF report, p. 86.
[58] Thondhlana, Barnabas. "Closure of Bureaux de Change to affect Forex liberalisation." *Zimbabwe Independent*, Jan. 2, 2003.
[59] ibid.
[60] *Financial Gazette*. "New Rules see Forex Inflows Plunge 70%" 1/16/2003.
[61] Thondlana, Barnabus. "Foreign currency deficit hits $660 million." The Zimbabwean Independent, December 13, 2002.
[62] ibid.
[63] Njanji, Susan. "No let up in Zimbabwe's forex woes as country fails to even print bank notes." Agence France Presse, May 11, 2003.
[64] Human Development Indicators 2003, United Nations Development Program (UNDP), at www.undp.org.
[65] Coakly, George, "The Mineral Industry of Zimbabwe", *U.S. Geological Survey Minerals Yearbook* (2001), p. 31.1.
[66] This calculation was done using the World Banks PPP measure of exchange rate, rather than the severely overvalued government's measure.
[67] Unattributed, "Zimbabwe's gold mines face closure" in *AfricaOnLine*, http://www.africaonline.com/site/Articles/1,3,53128.jsp
[68] Unattributed, "Gold mines face closure in Zimbabwe" in *Namibian*, http://www.namibian.com.na/2003/july/marketplace/03e9A77B1D.html.
[69] Coakly, p. 31.2.
[70] Unattributed, Chamber of Mines of Zimbabwe, p. 2. See http://www.chamines.co.zw/minerals.htm
[71] July 2003 IMF Country Report, p. 86.
[72] Quoted in "Zimbabwe's gold mines face closure", 8/26/03.
[73] July 2003 IMF Country Report, p. 8.
[74] Cited in *Futures and Commodity Market News*, 8/26/03, at http://news.tradingcharts.com/futures/0/6/39182960.html
[75] Cited in Coakly, p. 31.2.
[76] Ryan, Brendan, "Only Way Up Is Down", in *Financial Mail*, August 1, 2003. at http://free.financialmail.co.za/03/0801/busafrica/abusaf.htm.
[77] Unattributed, "Country Earns $70 bn From Gold and Platinum," in *The Daily News* (Harare), August 15, 2003, at http://allafrica.com/stories/200308150137.html
[78] Ibid.
[79] July 2003 IMF Country Report, 03/225, p. 8.
[80] IMF report, p. 67-70.
[81] IMF report, p. 69-72.
[82] IMF report, p. 67.
[83] IMF report, p. 67.
[84] WSJ article, Dec. 24, 2003.
[85] Reserve Bank of Zimbabwe.
[86] Mabika S E, http://www.resbank.co.za/Economics/Conference_Papers/zimbabwe.pdf.

Chapter six

[1] Riddell, p. 15.
[2] ibid, p. 25.
[3] ibid, p. 23.
[4] *Socioeconomic Review*, p. 173.

[5] *The Guardian*, "No Surrender." June 10, 2003.

[6] *Zimbabwe National Commission for UNESCO.* "The Developments in Education: The Education System At The End Of The 20th Century." Harare, July 2001. Available online at http://www.ibe.unesco.org/International/ICE/natrap/Zimbabwe.pdf.

[7] Davies and Sanders, p. 286.

[8] Sylvester, p. 124.

[9] *Socioeconomic Review*, p. 173, and 2001 UNESCO report on Education.

[10] *The Guardian*, "No Surrender", June 10, 2003. Available online at http://education.guardian.co.uk/print/0,3858,4687048-108234,00.html

[11] ibid.

[12] ibid.

[13] *Africa online*. "Zimbabwe's pride-education- on the rocks." December 18, 2002. Online at http://www.africaonline.com/site/Articles/1,3,51421.jsp

[14] ibid.

[15] World Bank, *Zimbabwe Population Sector Report* (Demographic Annex), p. 5.

[16] *Economist Intelligence Unit* (1990), p. 6.

[17] *Statistical Yearbook*, p. 15.

[18] *1982 Census of Zimbabwe*, p. 9.

[19] *Xinhua News Agency*, "Zimbabwe's Population Growth Slows Down." Sept. 20, 2001

[20] *Socioeconomic Review*, p. 163

[21] World Bank, Report 8100-ZIM, p. 1.

[22] *Socioeconomic Review*, p. 163.

[23] ibid, p. 166.

[24] ibid, p. 2.

[25] *Economist Intelligence Unit* (1989), p. 7,8.

[26] World Bank Report 8100-ZIM, p. 1.

[27] The World Bank, *World Atlas*, p. 9.

[28] Year 1988 comes from *World Development Report, 1990*. Year 1980, comes from *World Development Report, 1982*. Both reports were published by the World Bank.

[29] World Bank Report 8100-ZIM, p. 3.

[30] Key, Sandra, et. al, "AIDS cuts life expectancy of Zimbabwean Babies." *AIDS Weekly Plus*, 10/26/98.

[31] IMF Report, p. 30.

[32] *Precis*, "Meeting the Health Care Challenge in Zimbabwe." World Bank Operations Evaluations Department, Winter 1999, Number 176.

[33] ibid, p. 3.

[34] Key, Keith, "AIDS patients barred from kidney treatment facilities," in *AIDS Weekly Plus*, 3/4/96.

[35] Key, Sandra, "Country to punish deliberate HIV transmitters." *AIDS Weekly Plus*, 7/14/97.

[36] July 2003 IMF report, p. 31.

[37] ibid, p. 32.

[38] See *Private Choices and Public Health: The AIDS Epidemic in an Economic Perspective*, by Tomas Philipson and Richard Posner for an excellent discussion of this point. Harvard University Press (1993).

[39] Unattributed, "Fact Sheet- Young People at Risk: HIV/AIDS among America's Youth", Center for Disease Control, March 11, 2002. Available at: http://www.cdc.gov/hiv/pubs/facts/youth.htm.

[40] 1998 DHS Survey.

Chapter seven

[1] *Statistical Yearbook 1987*, p. 45.

[2] ibid, p. 45.

[3] Davies, p. 280.
[4] *Socioeconomic Review*, p. 101.
[5] ibid, p. 97.
[6] ibid, p. 95 and 101.
[7] Countrywatch.com, p.20.
[8] CNN.com. "Zimbabwe President Mugabe labels white farmers 'enemies', April 8, 2000.
[9] *Socioeconomic Review*, p. 103.
[10] *Statistical Yearbook 1985*, p. 44.
[11] *Statistical Yearbook 1987*, p. 48.
[12] Cited in Brand, Veronica, Rodreck Mupedziswa and Perpetua Gumbo, "Structural Adjustment, Women and Informal Trade in Harare." *Structural Adjustment and The Working Poor in Zimbabwe*, edited by Gibbons, Peter. Nordiska Afrikainstitutet, 1995.
[13] Mazur, pp. 5-7.
[14] Brand, p. 180.
[15] Brand, p. 182.
[16] Boserup, p. 22.
[17] ibid, p. 19.
[18] Kazembe, p. 380.
[19] ibid.
[20] Weinrich, p. 119.
[21] ibid.
[22] Kazembe, pp. 380 and 385.
[23] ibid, p. 389.
[24] ibid, p. 385.
[25] Mazur, p. 7.
[26] ibid, p. 391.
[27] ibid.
[28] ibid, p. 389.
[29] Unattributed, "Zimbabwe: Land Ownership Still Denied To Women." *Women's International Network News*, Winter 2001, Vol. 27, Issue 1, p. 66.

Chapter 8

[1] Everingham, Mark. "Agricultural Property Rights and Political Change in Nicargua." *Latin American Politics and Society*, vol. 43, no. 3 (Fall). #1.
[2] ibid.
[3] ibid.
[4] World Bank, "Nicaraguan Poverty Assessment: Challenges and Opportunities for Poverty Reduction." 2001.
[5] Thiesenhusen, W., Hendrix, S., "Poverty and Progress: The cases of El Salvador and Nicaragua." *Harvard International Review*, 07391854, Spring95, Vol. 17, Issue 2.
[6] Williams, Philip. 1994. Dual Transitions from Authoritarian Rule: Popular and Electoral Democracy in Nicaragua. *Comparative Politics* 26, 2: 169-85.
[7] Neira, Oscar, "The IMF and Financial-Sector Reform in Nicaragua." at www.developmentgap.org.
[8] Gonzalez, David. "Among Unpaid Wages of a Revolution: Competing Claims on Land in Nicaragua." *The New York Times*, Sept. 10. 2000.
[9] ibid.
[10] Stanfield, cited in Everingham.
[11] Everingham, Mark..
[12] Gonzalez, Sept. 10, 2000.
[13] ibid.

[14] *World Bank Country Brief.* on Nicaragua, 1999.
[15] ibid.
[16] Theisenhusen and Hendrix.
[17] *World Bank Country Brief* on Nicaragua, 1999.
[18] *World Bank Press Release No. 98/7.* "IMF Approves Three-Year Arrangement Under ESAF for Nicaragua." March 19, 1998.
[19] LaFraniere, Sharon, "Africa Quandary: Whites' Land Vs. the Landlessness of Blacks." in *The New York Times*, Jan. 6, 2004, p. A1.
[20] Haber, Stephen, Douglass C. North and Barry R. Weingast. "If Economists Are So Smart, Why Is Africa So Poor?" in *The Wall Street Journal.* (Eastern edition). New York, N.Y.: Jul 30, 2003. pg. A12
[21] Zachary, Pascal. "How Dutch Defend Hearth and Home By Sleeping Around --- Amsterdam's `Antisquatters' Pay To Occupy Vacant Buildings And Keep the Riffraff Away" *The Wall Street Journal.* (Eastern edition). New York: Mar 23, 1999. pg. A.1
[22] According to Nationmaster, an Internet database that collects international data, Zimbabwe has 5 murders per 100,000 people; the United States has 3 per 100,000. South Africa is the world's highest, at 73 per 100,000, followed by Colombia, at 53 per 100,000. Available at: http://www.nationmaster.com/red/graph-T/cri_mur_wit_fir_cap&int=20.
[23] Haber, Stephen,et. al. used the phrase "thorny" in this context.
[24] Friedman, Milton, in *Capitalism and Freedom*, p. 15.
[25] Countrywatch.com, Zimbabwe review, p. 70.
[26] O Rouke, Breffni, "EU: How Ireland Unleashed Its 'Celtic Tiger' Economy (Part 1)" published by *Radio Free Europe*, November 26, 2001. Available at: http://www.rferl.org/nca/features/2001/11/26112001091243.asp.

Bibliography

Africa News Service. "WFP Warns of Disaster in Zimbabwe." December 7, 2002.

AfricaOnLine (unattributed). "Zimbabwe's gold mines face closure," available at: http://www.africaonline.com/site/Articles/1,3,53128.jsp.

Alston, Lee J., Gary D. Libecap and Robert Schneider. "The Determinants and Impact of Property Rights: Land Titles on the Brazilian Frontier." *Journal of Law,* Economics, and Organization, 12(1), 25-61 (1996).

Alwang, Jeffery, Bradford Mills and Nelson Taruvinga. "Why Has Poverty Increased in Zimbabwe?" Washington, D.C. *World Bank Poverty Dynamics in Africa Series*, March 2002.

Baker, J., "Rural Communities Under Stress: Peasant Farmers and the State in Africa." Cambridge: Cambridge University Press, 1989.

Barro, Robert J. "Economic Growth in a Cross Section of Countries." *Quarterly Journal of Economics*, Vol. 106 (1991), pp. 406-443.

Bate, Roger, "Culling to be Kind," The Competitive Enterprise Institute, March 16, 1999, available at http://www.cei.org/gencon/004.01572.cfm.

Bijlmakers, L. Mary Bassett and David Sanders, "Health and Structural Adjustment in Rural and Urban Settings in Zimbabwe. Some Interim Findings." in *Structural Adjustment and the Working Poor in Zimbabwe*, edited by Peter Gibbon. Uppsala: Nordiska Africkinstitutet, 1995.

Billing, K.J. "Zimbabwe and the CGIAR Centers: A Study of Their Collaboration in Agricultural Research," CGIAR Study Paper #6. Washington, DC: The World Bank, 1985.

Block, Fred. "Political Choice and Multiple 'Logics' of Capital." *Theory and Society,* 15:175-92 (1986).

Bongarts, John and Potter, Robert G. *Fertility, Biology and Behavior, An Analysis of Proximate Determinants,* New York: Academic Press, NY,1983.

Boserup, Ester, *Woman's Roles in Economic Development.* Aberdeen (Great Britain): Aberdeen University Press, 1972.

Broegaard, Rikke J., Rasmus Heltberg, and Nikolaj Malchow-Moller. "Property Rights and Land Tenure in Nicaragua." Center for Development Research working paper.

Bruce, J.W., Fortmann, L. and Nhira, C. "Tenures in Transition, Tenures in Conflict: Examples for the Zimbabwean Social Forest." *Rural Sociology,* 54(4), (1993):626-42.

Bulatao, Rudolfo, Edward Bos, Patience Stephens and My Vu.. *Africa Region Population Projections*, 1989-90 Edition. Population and Human Resources Department, Washington, DC: The World Bank, November 1989.

Campbell, John L., Lindberg, Leon. "Property Rights and the Organization of Economic Activity by the State." *American Sociological Review,* October (1990).

Center for Disease Control. "Fact Sheet-Young People at Risk: HIV/AIDS among America's Youth," http://www.cdc.gov/hiv/pubs/facts/youth.htm.

Central Statistical Office. *Supplement to the Monthly Digest of Statistics, January, 1980.* Salisbury,Zimbabwe: 1980.

Central Statistical Office, and The Institute for Resource Development/Macro Systems (Columbia, MD). *Zimbabwe Demographic and Health Survey in 1988 (DHS 1988)..* Harare: 1989.

______________________. *Quarterly Digest of Statistics*. December. Harare: 1988.

______________________ *Zimbabwe, Statistical Yearbook 1987* .Harare, Zimbabwe: 1985.

Chamber of Mines of Zimbabwe (unattributed), various data, available at http://www.chamines.co.zw/minerals.htm

Chitepo, Witness. "Zimbabwe: Rushing Backwards." *African Business,* September 2002.

Clark, D.G. "The Distribution of Income and Wealth in Rhodesia," *Mambo Occasional Papers, Socioeconomic Series #7*, Rhodesia: Mambo Press, 1977.

CNN.com. "Zimbabwe's President Mugabe labels white farmers 'enemies'," April 8, 2000.

Coakly, George. "The Mineral Industry of Zimbabwe." in *U.S. Geological Survey Minerals Yearbook*, 2001.

Cochrane, Susan, *Fertility and Education: What Do We Really Know?* World Bank Staff Occasional Papers, #26: (1979).

Countrywatch.com. *Zimbabwe: 2003 Country Review.* Available online.

Dashwood, Hevina. *Zimbabwe: The Political Economy of Transformation.* Toronto: University of Toronto Press, 2000.

da Silva, Vicky. "The Land Issue in Zimbabwe." published online by the Electoral Institute of Southern Africa (eisa.org.za). February 25, 2002.

Davies, Rob and Sanders, David. "Adjustment Policies and the Welfare Children: Zimbabwe, 1980-1985 in *Adjustment with a Human Face*, Vol. II: 1987.

de Soto, Hernando. *The Mystery of Capital,* New York: Basic Books, 2000.

Dempster, Carolyn. "Zimbabwe's Changed Land." BBC News, http://news.bbc.co.uk, February 28, 2003.

Everingham, Mark. "Agricultural Property Rights and Political Change in Nicaragua." *Latin American Politics and Society,*(Fall 2001), vol. 43, no. 3.

Farid, Samir. "Fertility in Sub-Saharan Africa." A World Bank Discussion Paper #43. Washington, D.C. The World Bank, 1989. *FASonline*. "Zimbabwe: Drought Threatens 2001/02 Summer Crops." February 20, 2002, at http://www.fas.usda.gov/pecad2/highlights/2002/02/zim/zimfeb.htm

Feder, Gershon. "Access to Land and Poverty Reduction". Presentation at the International Colloquium for Agrarian Reform and Rural Development in the 21st Century, Puebla, Mexico, December 6-8, 1999.

Feder, G., Onchan, T., Chalamwong, Y. and Hongladarom, C. *Land Policies and Farm Productivity in Thailand.* World Bank, Baltimore: The Johns Hopkins University Press, 1998.

Ferguson, Niall. *Empire.* New York: Basic Books, 2002.

Financial Gazette. "The Costs of Parallel Exchange Rates." January 17, 2002.

_______________. "New Rules See Forex Inflows Plunge 70%." January 16, 2003.

Food and Agricultural Organization. "Special Report: FAO/WFP Crop and Food Supply Assessment Mission to Zimbabwe." May 29th, 2002, pp. 1-3, at http://www.fao.org/docrep/005/y6816e/y6816e00.htm.

Friedman, Milton, *Capitalism and Freedom.* Chicago: University of Chicago Press, 1962.

Gann, Lewis and Henriksen, T.H. *The Struggle for Zimbabwe.* New York: Praeger Publishers, 1981.

Glaser, Mark. "Zimbabwe's *Daily News* Fights Closure with Online Publication." *USC Annenberg Online Journalism Review*, 10/22/2003. Available at: http://www.ojr.org/ojr/glaser/1066860746.php.

Godwin, Peter. "A Land Possessed." *National Geographic,* August 2003.

Goldsmith, Arthur A. "Democracy, Property rights and Economic growth." *Journal of Development Studies*, Dec. (1995), v32, p. 157 (18).

Gonzalez, David. "Among Unpaid Wages of a Revolution: Competing Claims on Land in Nicaragua." *The New York Times*, September 10, 2000.

Granovetter, Mark. "Economic Action and Social Structure: The Problem of Embeddedness," *American Journal of Sociology*, 91 (1985): 481-510.

Griffin, Charles C., "Changes in the Provision of Health Services in Chile and Zimbabwe," excerpted from "Strengthening Health Services in Developing Countries through the Private Sector," an International Finance Corporation publication (affiliated with the World Bank).

Grossman, Gene and Elhanan Helpnan. *Innovation and Growth in the Global Economy.* Cambridge, Mass: MIT Press, 1991.

Haber, Stephen; North, Douglass C., Weingast, Barry R. "If Economists Are So Smart, Why is Africa So Poor?" *Wall Street Journal,* (Eastern edition), New York, NY: July 30, 2003, pg. A12.

Heltberg, R. "Rural Market Failures and the Farm Size - Productivity Relationship: Evidence from Pakistan", *World Development (1998)*, 26(10): 1807-26.

Hill, Ryan and Katarere, Yemi, "Colonialism and Inequity in Zimbabwe," IUCN report: Harare: 2001.

House, John and Margaret. *Zimbabwe, A Handbook*. Harare: Mercury Press Ltd., 1983.

Human Development Indicators 2003, United Nations Development Program (UNDP), at www.undp.org.

International Monetary Fund. *Zimbabwe: 2003 Article IV Consultation- Staff Report.* Washington, DC: IMF Publication Services, July 2003.

IRINNEWS.org. "EU names Zimbabwe's blacklist." published online by the United Nations Office for Coordination of Human Affairs. July 25, 2002.

_______________. "MDC set to challenge election result." April 10, 2002.

_______________. "Zimbabwe: By-election marred by allegations of foul play." October 28, 2002.

_______________. "Bombing of radio office condemned." August 29, 2002.

Kadhari, Xavier. "The Economy: Issues, Problems and Prospects," in *Zimbabwe-The Political Economy of Transition 1980-1986,* edited by Ibbo Mandaza. Dakar, Senegal: CODESRIA Press, 1986.

Kazembe, Joyce, "The Women Issue," in *Zimbabwe-The Political Economy of Transition 1980-1986,* edited by Ibbo Mandaza. Dakar, Senegal: CODESRIA Press, 1986.

Key, Keith. "AIDS patients barred from kidney treatment facilities." in *AIDS Weekly Plus*. 3/4/96.

Key, Sandra. "Country to punish deliberate HIV transmitters." *AIDS Weekly Plus*. 7/14/97.

Key, Sandra. "AIDS cuts life expectancy of Zimbabwean Babies." *AIDS Weekly Plus*. 10/26/98.

Knight, Frank.H. *Risk, Uncertainty and Profit*. Chicago: University of Chicago Press, 1971.

Kundhlande, G. and Luckert, M.K. "Towards an Analytical Framework for Assessing Property Rights to Natural Resources: A Case Study in the Communal Areas of Zimbabwe." Staff Paper, Department of Rural Economy, University of Alberta, 2000.

LaFraniere, Sharon. "Africa Quandary: Whites' Land vs. the Landlessness of Blacks," in *The New York Times,* January 6, 2004, p. A1.

La Porta, Rafael, Forencio Lopez-de-Silanes, Andreiano Shleifer, and Robert Vishny, "Law and Finance." *Journal of Political Economy,* 106/6 (1998), pp. 1113-55

Lee, Richard. "Crisis in Chidobe." *Zimbabwe Eyewitness*, World Food Program, at www.wfp.org/newsroom/in_depth/africa/sa_chidobe0209.htm

LOLApress Africa. "Zimbabwe: Land Ownership Still Denied to Women." Johannesburg, SA: *Women's International Network News*, Winter 2001, p. 66.

Lutz, Ernst, ed. "Agriculture and the environment: Perspectives on sustainable rural development", Washington, D.C.: World Bank, 1998.

Mabika, S.E., "Monetary Policy Framework in Zimbabwe. Reserve Bank of Zimbabwe Conference Paper, presented at The South AfricanReserveBank, September 17, 2001.

Maclean's (unattributed). "Land grab". Toronto: August 19th 2002.

Ministry of Finance, Economic Planning and Development. *Socioeconomic Review of Zimbabwe for 1980-1985*. Harare: 1986.

Moyo, Sam. "The Land Question." in *Zimbabwe-The Political Economy of Transition 1980-1986*, edited by Ibbo Mandaza,: Dakar, Senegal: CODESRIA Press, 1986.

Mumbengegwi, Clever. "Continuity and Change in Agricultral Policy," in *Zimbabwe-The Political Economy of Transition 1980-1986*, edited by Ibbo Mandaza. CODESRIA: Dakar, Senegal: 1986.

Mutambira, Jane. "Health Problems in Rural Communities, Zimbabwe." *Social Science and Medicine*, 29(8) (1989), pp. 927-932.

Namibian (unattributed). "Gold mines face closure in Zimbabwe." http://www.Namibian.com.na/2003/july/marketplace/03e9A77B1D.html.

Natsios, Andrew. "The Food Crisis in Southern Africa: The Challenge to Sustainability," reported at a USAID Foreign Press Briefing, on August 20, 2002.

Neira, Oscar. "The IMF and Financial-Sector Reform in Nicaragua." *The Development Group for Alternative Policies*, available at www.developmentgap.org.

Njanji, Susan. "No let up in Zimbabwe's forex woes as country fails to even print bank notes." *lAgence France Presse,* May 11, 2003.

North, Douglas. *Institutions, Institutional Change and Economic Performance.* Cambridge: Cambridge University Press.

Norton, Seth. "Poverty, Property Rights, and Human Well-Being: A Cross-National Study." *CATO Journal* (Fall 1998), Vol. 18, Issue 2.

Nyambara, Pius Shugudzapera. "The Politics of Land Acquisition and Struggles Over Land in the 'Communal' Areas of Zimbabwe: The Gokwe Region in the 1980s and the 1990s," *Africa* (2001), 71 (2).

Olson, Mancur. The Rise and Fall of Nations. New Haven, CT: Yale University Press, 1982.

O'Rourke, Breffni, "EU: How Ireland Unleashed its 'Celtic Tiger' Economy (Part 1)," published by *Radio Free Europe*, November 26, 2001, available at: http://www.rferl.org/nca/features/2001/11/26112001091243.asp.

Pana Daily News Wire, "Zimbabwe's Central Bank Tightens Foreign Exchange Rules," 11/25/2001.

Philipson, Tomas and Posner, Richard. *Private Choices and Public Health: The AIDS Epidemic in an Economic Perspective*. Cambridge: Harvard University Press, 1993.

ReliefWeb. "Zimbabwe: Drought takes toll on livestock", April 8, 2003.

Riddell, Roger. *Education for Employment.* London: Catholic Institute for International Relations, 1980.

Romer, Paul. "Increasing Returns and Economic Growth." *Journal of Political Economy 95* (October 1986): 1002-1037.

Ross, Doris, Arto Kovanen, Lodewyk Erasmus, Jay Surti, Gustavo Bagattini, Nadeem Ilahi and Helga Treichel. "Zimbabwe: Selected Issues and Statistical Appendix" *IMF Country Report No. 03/225.* Washington, D.C: The International Monetary Fund, July 2003.

Rosenberg, Nathan. *Exploring The Black Box: Technology, Economics and History.* Cambridge: Oxford University Press, 1994.

Rugube, L. and W. Chambati. "Broadening Access to Land Markets in Southern Africa." Madison, Wisconsin: The Land Tenure Center.

Ryan, Brendan, "Only Way Up Is Down," *Financial Mail,* August 1, 2003, at http://free financialmail.co.za/03/0801/busafrica/abusaf.htm.

Sachikonye, L.M. "Industrial Restructuring and Labour Relations," in *Structural Adjustment and the Working Poor in Zimbabwe (*edited by Peter Gibbon). Uppsala, Sweden: Nordiska Afrikainstitutet, 1995.

Scully, G. The Institutional Framework and Economic Development." *Journal of Political Economy.* (1988), vol. 96, pp. 652-62.

Scully, G. and D.J. Slottje. "Ranking Economic Liberty Across Countries." *Public Choice* (1991), vol. 69, pp. 121-52.

Skalnes, Tor. *The Politics of Economic Reform in Zimbabwe.* New York: St. Martin's Press, 1995.

Smith, Adam. *An Inquiry into the Nature and Origins of the Wealth of Nations.* New York: Modern Library, 1937.

Solow, Robert M. "A Contribution to the Theory of Economic Growth". *Quarterly Journal of Economics*, Vol. 70 (1956), pp. 65-94.

Stiglitz, Joseph. *Globalization and its Discontents.* New York: Norton and Company, 2003.

Sylvester, Christine. *Zimbabwe: The Terrain of Contradictory Development.* Boulder: Westview Press, 1991.

Tan, Jee Peng and Haines, Michael. "Schooling and Demand for Children." World Bank Staff Working Paper #697. Washington, D.C: The World Bank, 1984.

The Commonwealth of Learning (unattributed). The official website of the British Commonwealth, available at: www.col.org.

The Daily News (Zimbabwe), "Bulawayo City Council rules out water rationing," online edition, 5/12/02.

________________________. "Country Earns $70 bn from Gold and Platinum,." (Harare), August 15, 2003, online edition.

________________________. "Victory for *Daily News.*" online edition, January 4, 2004.

The Economist, "Zimbabwe, Success at Risk," April 22, 1989, pp. 21-23.

____________. "It's the King's Land, OK?" December 31, 1999, p. 16.

____________. "The Heart Of The Matter" May 13th, 2000, p. 22.

____________.. "Zimbabwe's Beans and Bicycles," February 17th, 2001, p. 49.

The Economist Intelligence Unit. Zimbabwe Country Report No. 2, 1990. London: 1990.

____________________________. Zimbabwe Country Profile 1989-90. London: 1989.

The Economist Intelligence Unit. . Zimbabwe Country Profile 1988-89. London: 1988.

Thiesenhusen, W., Hendrix, S. "Poverty and Progress: The cases of El Salvador and Nicaragua." *Harvard International Review,* (Spring 95), Vol. 17, Issue 2.

Thondhlana, Barnabas. "Closure of Bureaux de Change to Affect Forex Liberalisation." *Zimbabwe Independent,* January 2, 2003.

Thondhlana, Barnabas. "Foreign Currency Deficit Hits $660 Million." *Zimbabwe Independent,* December 13, 2002.

Thurow, Roger. "Once a Breadbasket, Zimbabwe Today Can't Feed Itself." *The Wall Street Journal*, December 24, 2003, p. A1.

Torstennson, Johan. "Property Rights and Economic Growth: An Empirical Study." *Kyklos* (1994), Vol. 47, Issue 2.

New York Times (unattributed author). "Zimbabwe to name thousands of blacks to get farms of whites." December 30, 2001.

UNESCO. *Basic Education and Literacy, World Statistical Indicators 1990.* New York: Office of Statistics, 1990.

Utting, Peter. *Bosques, sociedad y poder*. Managua, Universidad Centroamericana (UCA), 1996.

United Nations. *Demographic Yearbook 1980.* NY: United Nations Office, 1982.

United Nations. *World Population Prospects 1988.* NY: United Nations Office, 1989.

United Nations. *1990 Human Development Report.* NY: United Nations Office, 1990.

Weinrich, A.K.H., *Women and Racial Discrimination in Rhodesia*. Paris: UNESCO Press, 1979.

Williams, Philip. "Dual Transitions from Authoritarian Rule: Popular and Electoral Democracy in Nicaragua." *Comparative Politics.* (1994), 26, 2: 169-85.

Willmer, Tanya. "Commonwealth policy on Zim in tatters," online at *iafrica.com*, December 8, 2003.

Wines, Michael. "A Bleak Ride Home for Zimbabwe Deportees." *New York Times*, p. A1, col. 01, September 23, 2003.

Wilson, Derek. *The World Encompassed.* New York: Harper and Row, 1977.

World Bank. Report #PIC1101, "Zimbabwe-Structural Adjustment Loan III, internal report, 1994.

__________. "Zimbabwe Population Sector Report. *Main Report,* p. 11, p. 12.

__________. "Zimbabwe Land Subsector Study." *Southern Agricultural Division, Report 5878-ZIM*, 1986.

World Bank. Southern Africa Department, Population and Human Resources Division, *Zimbabwe Population Sector Report:* October 1989.

__________. various years. *World Development Report*. New York: Oxford University Press.

__________. "Economics of Tobacco Control," available online at http://www1.worldbank.org/tobacco/chapter5.asp.

__________. *Country Report on Nicaragua 1999*. Washington, D.C: World Bank Publications, 1999.

__________. *World Bank Atlas*. Washington, DC: World Bank publications, 1989.

__________. *World Development Indicators*. (online). Washington, D.C.: The World Bank, 2002.

__________. *World Development Report 1965*. The International Bank for Reconstruction and Development/The World Bank. New York: Oxford University Press, 1965.

__________. *World Development Report 1989*. The International Bank for Reconstruction and Development/The World Bank, New York: Oxford University Press, 1989.

__________. *World Development Report 1990*. The International Bank for Reconstruction and Development/The World Bank. New York: Oxford University Press, 1990.

__________. *World Tables 1988-1989*. Baltimore: Johns Hopkins University Press, 1989.

Zachary, Pascal. "How Dutch Defend Hearth and Home by Sleeping Around --- Amsterdam's 'Antisquatters' Pay to Occupy Vacant Buildings and Keep the Riffraff Away." *The Wall Street Journal*, (Eastern edition), New York, NY: July 30, 2003, pg. A12.

Zeilig, Leo."Crisis in Zimbabwe." *International Socialism Journal*, Issue 94, Spring 2002.

Zimbabwe National Planning Council, and Westinghouse Applied Systems. *Zimbabwe Reproductive Health Survey 1984*. Columbia, MD: 1985.

Zimbabwe National Planning Council. "Development of the Zimbabwe Family Planning Programme." Harare, Zimbabwe: 1990.

Zimbabwe Census Department. Main Demographic Features of the Population of Zimbabwe, An Advance Report Based on a Ten Percent Sample (1982 Population Census), Harare: June 1985.

Zvobgo, Rungano J. "Education and the Challenge for Independence," in *Zimbabwe-The Political Economy of Transition 1980-1986*, edited by Ibbo Mandaza. Dakar, Senegal, 1986.

Name Index

Alwang, Jeffrey 69
Beattie, Andrew 94
Block, Fred 14
Campbell, John L. 14
Chamorro, Violeta Barrios de 136-139, 145
De Soto, Hernando 4, 7, 18, 19, 23, 83
Drake, Francis 11
Everingham, Mark 136, 137
Friedman, Milton 44, 144
Goldsmith, Arthur 12-15
Granovetter, Mark 14
Grossman, Gene 14
Hernandez, Lino 140
Kay, Iain 79
Knight, Frank 15-16
Kubheka, Magaliso 142
Lindberg, Leon 14
Lobengula 27, 28
Luckert, M.K. 55
Made, Joseph 78
Makoni, Simba 91
Mangwende, Witness 37, 38
Masuko, Xolani 79
Moyo, Sam 53
Msika, Joseph 134
Mugabe, Robert 3, 4, 32-41, 43, 49, 70, 79, 108, 127
North, Douglas 15
Nyambara, Pius Shungudzapera 53
Ortega, Daniel 135
Prince, Stephen 58, photo captions
Queen Elizabeth I 11
Rhodes, Cecil 12, 28, 29, 42, 58
Romer, Paul 14
Rosenberg, Nathan 15
Sani, James 79
Scully, G. 15
Serima, Armando 79
Shepherd, Steve 97
Smith, Adam 7, 14, 16, 23
Smith, Ian 30-35, 43, 48, 49
Solow, Robert M. 14
Somoza, Anastasia 135
Tsvangirai, Morgan 39
William the Conquerer 11
Williams, Philip 138
Wright, Neil 47

Subject Index

AIDS,
  impact on Zimbabwe, 115-121
  treatment of, 116
Brideprice, 131,132
Britain, relations strained with Zimbabwe, 38
British South Africa Company, 12, 28
Buffalo, nearly extinct in U.S., 51
Central Bank of Nicaragua, actions of, 137,138
CFU. *See* Commercial Farmers' Union
Chamber of Mines, 96
Chamorro government, titling property, 138,139
Clinics, health, 116,117
Commercial Farmers' Union, 36,37 42,47,82
Commercial farms,
  ways of farming, 47,50
Commonwealth,
  Zimbabwe's suspension from, 43
Communal farmers,
  ways of farming, 47,50
Communal Lands Act, 42, 53
Conservative Alliance of Zimbabwe, 35
Contracts, protection of private property, 12
Cotton Marketing Board, 64
Current account, swings to red, 89
Dead capital, 4, 18, 83
Declaration of Rights, 45
Derelict Lands Board, 35
Devillefarm,
  in the Mazowe Valley, 78,79
Divorce, ability for women to, 132
Drought, 2001-02 in southern Africa, 70-74
Economic growth models, 14
Economic Structural Adjustment Program, 8, 65, 67-70
Education system,
  history of, 107-109
  costs to government, 109,110
  and its collapse, 111-113
Elephants, poaching and property rights in Zimbabwe, 51
England,
  history of property rights 11
  relationship to U.S, 13
  world's empire, 12
Enrollments,
  in educational paths, 107
ESAP. *See* Economic Structural Adjustment Program
European Union
  sanctions extended, 43
External payments arrears, 88
Fast Track program
  of land reform, 39-41
Food exports, 41
Foreign exchange outlets, role in currency shortage, 91, 92

Foreign exchange, from farming, 79-81
Formal sector, 128-129
French revolution,
 fight for property rights, 57
Gokwe district,
 study of communal farms, 53
Gold,
 production, 92,93
 price support scheme, 94
 Rhodes' discovery of, 28
 source of foreign exchange, 92
Government structure,
 comparison to U.S., 44
Grain Marketing Board (GMB), 64
 deficits, 65
Guilt, monitoring device in villages, 57
Health care,
 investment in, 115-117
 provision by Mugabe government prior to 2000, 116
Health expenditure,
 percent of GNP, 118
House of Assembly, 44
Human rights, disregard for, 35
IMPLATS, 97,98
Informal sector, 128
Jina village, case study of property rights laws, 56-57
Labor force, structure of, 125
Lancaster House Agreement, 36
Lancaster House Constitution, 34
Land Acquisition Act, 35, 37, 40, 42
Land ownership, inequities between blacks and whites, 47
Land rights, in villages, 56-58
Land seizures, 3, 4, 7, 8, 9, 42, 46, 75, 85, 113, 127
Life expectancy, drop in, 117
Literacy test, black vs. whites, 30
Local government, workings of, 46
Maize, staple crop of Zimbabwe, 59, 64, 68, 75-78
MDC. *See* Movement for Democratic Change
Meteorology Department of Zimbabwe, 71, 72
Ministry of Agricultural Development and Agrarian Reform (MIDINRA), 135, 136
Movement for Democratic Change, 39
Mozambique, 32, 51, 88
National Farmers Association of Zimbabwe (NFAZ), 50, 66
National government,
 workings of, 44, 45
Ndebele tribe, 27, 28, 30
NFAZ, *See* Zimbabwe National Farmers' Association of Zimbabwe
Nicaragua Chamorro government,
 treatment of property rights, 138-140
 external debt, 141
 inflation and economic growth, 137
 tariffs dropped, 138
North Korea,
 brutal regime, 44
Occupational classifications,
 men vs. women, 129
Over-invoicing in
 foreign exchange, 86
Parallel exchange rate, 86-92
Peru, labor supply effects
 of restored property rights, 19
Platinum ore deposits,
 huge discovery of, 97, 98
Price controls,
 in farming economy, 64-67
 placed on consumer goods, 88
Production differences,
 communal vs. commercial farms, 60

Property rights,
  and economic growth, 15, 16
  and work initiative, 16
  consequences of insecurity , 142
  Chamorro government
    treatment of, 138-140
  communal lands, 51-58
  economic models, 14
  British "exporting" to to
    other countries,
  flagrant disregard by
    Mugabe government, 3
  history of in England, 11
  history of in Zimbabwe, 27
  Lancaster House agreement, 36
  laws, 17
  limits in villages, 56-58
  literature review, 14, 15
  role in equity markets, 17
  water basins, 59
  trampled on in Nicaragua, 132
  willing seller-willing buyer
    clause, 37
  World Bank impact, 62
Property titles, lack of after land
  seizures, 83
Rainfall in Zimbabwe, 70-74
RBZ (Reserve Bank of Zimbabwe),
  93-95, 101-105
Rhodesian Front (RF), 30, 32
Risky sexual behavior and AIDS,
  121
Rudd Concession, 28
Sabbukku, chief of village, 52-56
Senate of Zimbabwe, 44
Shona tribe, 27, 28, 34
Somoza dictatorship
  of Nicaragua, 135
Supreme Court, rulings on land
  seizures, 40
Teachers, hiring in Zimbabwe, 108
The Daily Mail (Zimbabwe),
  shut down by government, 43
The Economist,
  journalist forced to leave, 43
The Nicaraguan Institute of Agrarian
  Reform (INRA), 137-138
Tobacco,
  changes in production, 59, 60
  percent of exports, 87
Tragedy of the commons, 51
  in communal lands, 58
UDI. *See* Unilateral declaration of
  independence
Underemployment,
  the problem of, 110
Under-invoicing,
  foreign exchange, 86
Unemployment, 113
Unilateral Declaration of
  Independence, 30, 31
United States,
  transition of property rights,
    13, 14
VIDCO
  (village development
  committee), 53
Wages
  trends in, by race, 126
Water
  access in sub-Saharan Africa,
    50-62
  precious resource for farming, 60
Women
  brideprice, 131
  legal remedies, 132-134
  social status of, 131
  role as family providers, 130
World Bank
  loans to Britain, 31
  peddling influence, 60
  suspension of disbursements, 88
  Zimbabwe's loss of
    voting rights, 70
World Food Program, 70, 71
Zambia, 32
ZANU/ZANU-PF, *See* Zimbabwe
  African National Union
ZAPU. *See* Zimbabwe African
  People's Union

Zimbabwe African People's
Union, 29
Zimbabwe African National Union,
31-35
Zimbabwe National Farmers'
Association of Zimbabwe
(NFAZ), 50
ZIMPLATS, 97, 98

STUDIES IN AFRICAN ECONOMIC AND SOCIAL DEVELOPMENT

1. Richard Vengroff and Alan Johnston, **Decentralization and the Implementation of Rural Development in Senegal**
2. Olayiwola Abegunrin, **Economic Dependence and Regional Cooperation in Southern Africa: SADCC and South Africa in Confrontation**
3. Charles O. Chikeka, **Britain, France, and the New African States: A Study of Post-Independence Relationships, 1960-1985**
4. Daniel Teferra, **The Making and Economy of Ethiopia**
5. Santosh Saha, **A History of Agriculture in Liberia, 1822-1970: Transference of American Values**
6. Santosh Saha, **A History of Agriculture in West Africa: A Guide to Information Sources**
7. Kwaku Osei-Hwedie, **A Search for Legitimate Social Development Education and Practice Models for Africa**
8. Emmanuel Ike Udogu, **Nigeria and the Politics of Survival as a Nation-State**
9. Aloy Chife, **The Political Economy of Post-Cold War Africa**
10. Benjamin Kline, **Profit, Principle and Apartheid, 1948-1994: The Conflict of Economic and Moral Issues in United States-South African Relations**
11. Senyo B-S. K. Adjibolosoo and Benjamin Ofori-Amoah (eds.), **Addressing Misconceptions About Africa's Development: Seeing Beyond the Veil**
12. Yaw Oheneba-Sakyi, **Female Autonomy, Family Decision Making, and Demographic Behavior in Africa**, with contributions from Kofi Awusabo-Asare
13. Michael Nana Osei-Mensah, **The Ghana Reform Case in African Technology and Telecommunications Policy**
14. Kelechi Amihe Kalu, **Economic Development and Nigerian Foreign Policy**
15. Kenneth Kaoma Mwenda, **Zambia's Stock Exchange and Privatisation Programme: Corporate Finance Law in Emerging Markets**
16. Henry W. West, **On African Land Holding–A Review of Tenurial Change and Land Policies in Anglophone Africa**
17. Mathurin C. Houngnikpo and Henry Kyambalesa, **Problems Facing Contemporary Africa and Viable Strategies for Redress**
18. Gaim Kibreab, **State Intervention and the Environment in Sudan, 1889-1989: The Demise of Communal Resource Management**
19. Ambe J. Njoh, **Self-Help Water Supply in Cameroon–Lessons on Community Participation in Public Works Projects**
20. Matthew Todd Bradley, **Nigeria Since Independence and the Impact of Non-Governmental Organizations on Democratization**
21. Chuka Onwumechili, **Reform, Organizational Players, and Technological Developments in African Telecommunications–An Update**
22. Kelfala Morana Kallon, **The Political Economy of Corruption in Sierra Leone**
23. Charles O. Chikeka, **European Hegemony and African Resistance, 1880-1990**
24. Craig Richardson, **The Collapse of Zimbabwe in the Wake of the 2000-2003 Land Reforms**